AN INTRODUCTION
TO THE ARCHITECTURAL
HERITAGE *of*

COUNTY
CAVAN

An Roinn
Ealaíon, Oidhreachta agus Gaeltachta
**Department of
Arts, Heritage and the Gaeltacht**

An Introduction to the Architectural Heritage of County Cavan

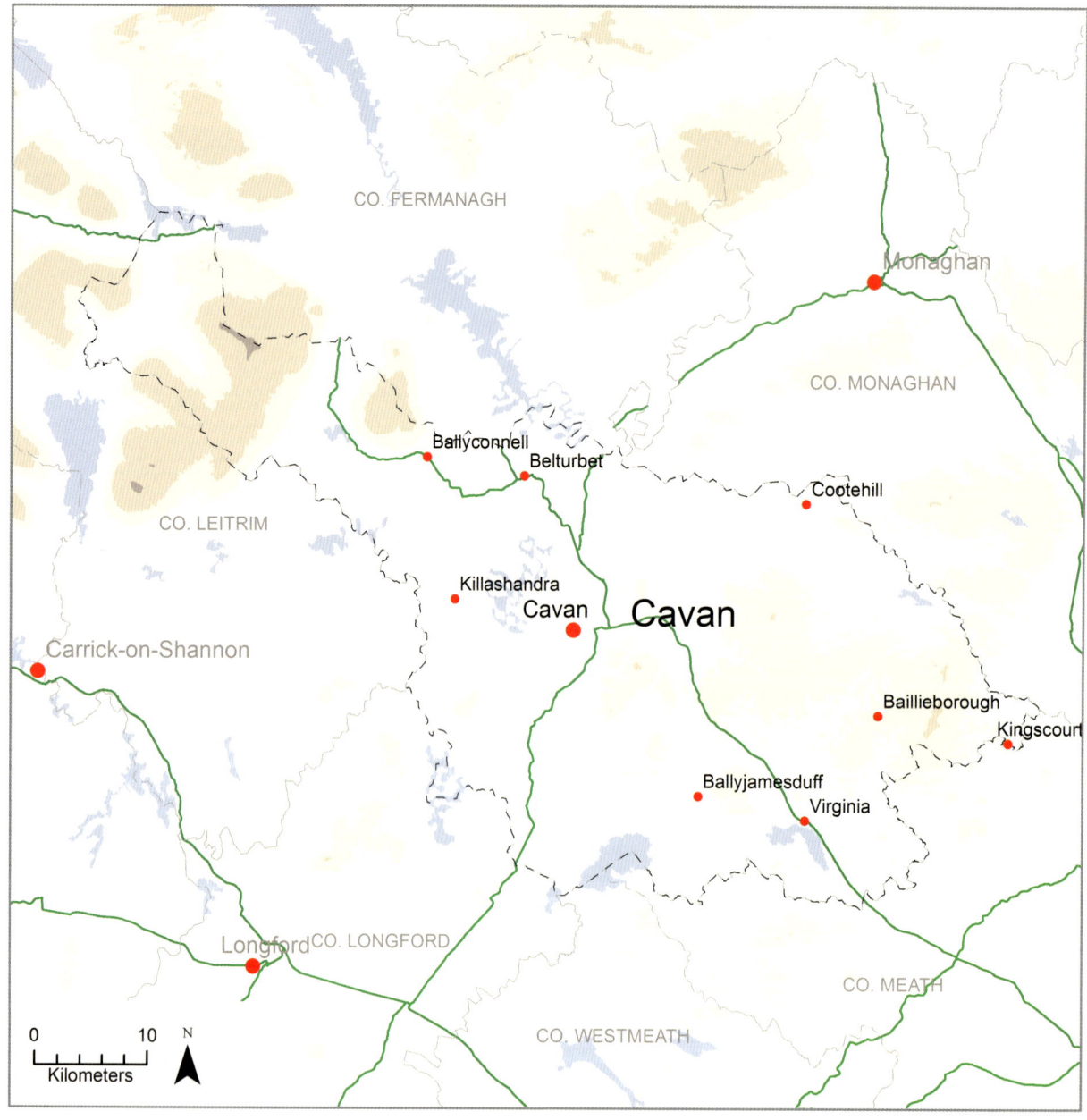

Foreword

The Architectural Inventory of County Cavan was carried out in 2012. A total of 860 structures were recorded. Of these some 770 are deemed worthy of protection.

The Inventory should not be regarded as exhaustive as, over time, other buildings and structures of merit may come to light. The purpose of the Inventory and of this Introduction is to explore the social and historical context of the buildings and to facilitate a greater appreciation of the built heritage of County Cavan.

The NIAH survey of the architectural heritage of County Cavan can be accessed on the internet at:
www.buildingsofireland.ie

NATIONAL INVENTORY
of ARCHITECTURAL HERITAGE

An Introduction to the Architectural Heritage *of* County Cavan

CUILCAGH LANDSCAPE

In contrast to the predominant drumlin landscape of Cavan, wilder, exposed landscapes characterise the long and narrow western portion of the county, with great expanses of blanket upland bogs contrasted against the prominent outline of Cuilcagh, part of the Cuilcagh Mountain range shared with county Fermanagh.

Introduction

Cavan is the most southerly county of Ulster. Its elongated figure brings it into contact with six neighbouring counties: Monaghan defines the east and north-east boundaries, Longford, Westmeath and Meath the south, while the distinctive panhandle that constitutes the north-west extremity is hemmed in by Fermanagh to the north and Leitrim to the south. The predominant drumlin landscape offers pleasing contrasts between gentle hills and the abundant surface water that makes Cavan one of the greatest lakeland districts in Ireland.

Rising in the centre of the county the River Erne flows south-west to Lough Gowna, spilling over the Longford border before continuing northwards to seep through the hills between Killeshandra and Cavan, puddling here to form Lough Oughter as an extensive lake. This intricate sequence of lake and river extends to Belturbet and beyond to Fermanagh, where it issues into the great expanses of Lough Erne. This central lakeland, which has been important for communication since earliest times, divides a benign, generally well wooded and highly picturesque landscape from the exposed mountain wildernesses to the north-west. Here the thinly populated countryside is characterised by poor lands with bleak open vistas, relieved only by numinous mountain presences, along the northern boundary by Slieve Rushen and Cuilcagh, its peak at 665 metres shared with Fermanagh, and further south by the domed profiles of Benbrack and Slievenakilla. Amidst these uplands lies the cradle of the Shannon, a deep pool at Legnashinna ('hollow of the Shannon') marking the origins of the country's longest river. Settlements in this remote region are few and represent the smallest in the county, including Dowra on the Shannon, Blacklion at the most northerly tip and Swanlinbar further west. Once a thriving eighteenth-century town, its fortune derived from the therapeutic waters produced by the iron-rich geology of the district.

Cavan, the county town, historically a Gaelic settlement at the heart of the highly-developed O'Reilly lordship of east Bréifne, continues to occupy a central position in the most fertile portion of the county. Throughout the surrounding countryside, and for most of the county, the small farm landscape of the drumlin belt prevails, the hills traversed by a chaotic interlace of small roads and rutted lanes that communicate between small fields and farmhouses, occasionally converging on one of the well-dispersed market towns and villages that remain highly dependent on the local agricultural economy.

While the slow unfolding character of the Cavan landscape and its picturesque lakelands have contributed greatly to the setting of its built heritage, the geology of the county has also bestowed a rich building tradition, offering a fitting diversity to the building stones of the county. Slate dominates, found as a blueish fine textured stone in the north-east around Cootehill, changing to a greener hue closer to Cavan town and altogether less fine and highly

WOODLAWN
Crover
(c.1800)

In the centre of the county, a combination of good land and the scenic qualities of its lakes accounts for the concentration of small landed estates like those that ring the shores of Lough Sheelin.

HOUSE
Coppanagh
(c.1810)

The glacial deposition which created the drumlin landscape, offered an abundance of freely available stone and clay which, being easily extracted from the ground, provided the basic structural material for most of the vernacular buildings in the county.

crystalline further south towards Virginia. Because it was easily cleft, it was widely used on buildings either as thinly coursed masonry for walls or for a time as roofing slate with numerous quarries for this purpose in evidence in the nineteenth century at Ballynahaia, east of Cootehill. Lower Carboniferous formations include the outcrop of older Devonian sandstones at Slieve Rushen and close to Cavan town a nineteenth-century quarry at Latt provided an attractive pale sandstone that was used to such good effect throughout the town, and at its finest in the ashlar work provided for its courthouse. The Carboniferous limestone that characterises much of north Leinster encroaches on the district around Lough Sheelin where the former quarries at Ross and at Carrick supplied material over a wide area for use in building work.

From the beginning of the modern age Cavan was located as a nexus between three provinces, and until the sixteenth century it was considered part of Connacht; its peripheral position has always defined its history and culture and, being on the edge of Ulster, its close relationship with Leinster made it the most permeable frontier to the otherwise unassailable northern province, open to influences that helped establish the richness and diversity of its built heritage.

ST JOSEPH'S CHURCH
Corlea
(c.1840)

The drumlins of south Cavan provide a landscape of pleasing contrasts that contributes to the distinctiveness of its built heritage.
Courtesy Kevin Mulligan

DOWRA BRIDGE
Dowra
(c.1860)

The landscape of Cavan is characterised by abundant surface water. The Shannon, which begins in a deep pool beneath the Cuilcagh Mountains, passes through Dowra on its long journey to the sea.

(fig.1)
DRUMLANE
Milltown
(Sixth century)

A sixth-century foundation traditionally associated with Saints Columba and Maedoc, the round tower, an icon of the Irish monastic tradition described in the Irish annals as Cloictheach or 'bell house', is represented here by a late eleventh or early twelfth-century example.
*Courtesy Photographic Unit,
Dept AHG*

Pre 1700

DUAL TOMB
Cohaw
(Neolithic period)

The earliest stone structures in Cavan were ambitious prehistoric monuments built by the first people to settle here, Neolithic farmers who overcame the challenges of the landscape to establish a viable society and who, in choosing to commemorate their ancestors with megalithic tombs, were part of a great western European tradition.
Courtesy Photographic Unit, Dept AHG

RINGFORT
Drummully East
(c.800)

Cavan is rich in both ringforts - earthen embankments which from the early Iron Age to the early Christian period secured the typical farmstead – and in crannogs, island settlements built partly in response to the unique local environment.
Courtesy Photographic Unit, Dept AHG

Modern Cavan was once part of the ancient territory of Bréifne, out of which two petty kingdoms had evolved by the thirteenth century - west Bréifne ruled by the O'Rourkes (Uí Ruairc), and east by the O'Reillys (Uí Raghallaigh). The important early Christian site at Drumlane *(fig.1)* has been associated with the earliest O'Reilly centre of power and according to tradition represented the boundary between the two Bréifnes. Another round tower existed south of Ballyconnell at Mullynagolman, for which only a curious exhibitionist figure survives, now in Tomregan parish church and believed to have originated over the tower doorway. Further evidence for the early Christian church in Cavan rests in a small number of sites where the few standing remains are all of later medieval origin.

As one of numerous minor lordships on the southern fringe of Ulster, east Bréifne was an important frontier defining the limit of Anglo-Norman penetration into the province.

(fig.2)
CLOUGHOUGHTER CASTLE
Lough Oughter
(Thirteenth century)

A View of Cloughoughter Castle, by William Ashford, c.1790. A robust limestone castle on a small artificial island, it rises impressively to just under 19 metres. Its defensive form is enhanced by narrow loops pierced through the great thickness of the walls and by regular embrasures along its parapet.
Courtesy Irish Heritage Trust

TRINITY ISLAND
Lough Oughter
(Founded 1237)

This remote church on an island in Lough Oughter was founded by Cathal O'Reilly. The Hiberno-Romanesque doorway at Kilmore is traditionally believed to have originated here. The bell-cote and pointed window to the west gable can be dated to the early fifteenth century when indulgences were granted towards the cost of restoration.
Courtesy Photographic Unit, Dept AHG

Evidence that it was a permeable frontier is demonstrated in the construction of motte and bailey castles at Knockatemple, Moybologue, Relagh Beg and Castle Rahan, which represent some of the early incursions of the de Lacys who, as overlords of Meath, attempted to extend their reach northwards before the end of the twelfth century. Essentially surviving as the earthwork foundations for timber-built defences and buildings, these sites represent the limit of Anglo-Norman expansion in the area which is likely to have been curtailed in part by the poorer characteristics of the land further north, considered too poor to support a stable manorial society. Two additional mottes, erected later by Walter de Lacy at Kilmore and Belturbet, appear to have been considered more for security reasons than as part of any initiative to settle permanently in Ulster.

The enduring symbol of the Anglo-Norman conquest however is the castle, and though rare in this region, one of the earliest examples in Ireland is the great circular keep of Clough Oughter *(fig.2)*, built in 1220, again for strategic reasons, by Walter de Lacy after he received the submission of the Uí Raghallaigh. It soon passed into the hands of the O'Reillys who held it securely until the early seventeenth century. Less is known about another, slightly smaller, tower in the north western extremity of the county, its existence now represented only by its circular foundations on Port Island in Lough McNean.

(fig.3)
KILMORE OLD CATHEDRAL
Kilmore Upper
(Thirteenth century)

Composed as a series of deep diminishing arches with chevron ornaments and dog-toothed voussoirs, the Kilmore design acknowledges its European architectural sources in the use of engaged shafts to the three outer orders, each with richly carved capitals and bases.

With the development of the region left largely in the hands of the O'Reilly chiefs and their supporters, the principal display of outside architectural influence continues primarily in ecclesiastical buildings. Reform of the early-medieval Irish church introduced religious orders to Ireland, and was especially evident in the spread of the Augustinian rule. In the mid-twelfth century canons from Kells travelled north to undertake the re-organisation of the monastery at Drumlane. Reflecting continental influences the church plan was elongated to provide for a chancel, separated from the nave by a long-lost timber screen. Another Augustinian foundation with an elongated plan was the Praemonstratensian priory of the Holy Trinity, founded in 1237 on an island in Lough Oughter. Similar plan proportions combined with a preference for island or lakeside sites characterises many of the medieval church ruins in Cavan, further exemplified by St Mogue's church in Templeport and Termon on the edge of Lough McNean. Generally the simple understated nature of the architecture means precise dating is difficult. However the small church beside Lough Annagh near Belturtbet is distinguished principally for its complete thirteenth-century cusped lancet window; set in the east gable, it is a rare survivor, externally quite simple with a hood-moulding but finer internally where a slender carved shaft with bell capital defines the angle of the splays. The greatest monument of the early medieval period is undoubtedly the richly decorated Hiberno-Romanesque doorway at Kilmore *(fig.3)* now incorporated into the Victorian cathedral. Its exact origins remain unclear, most likely from an early church at Kilmore given that its name,

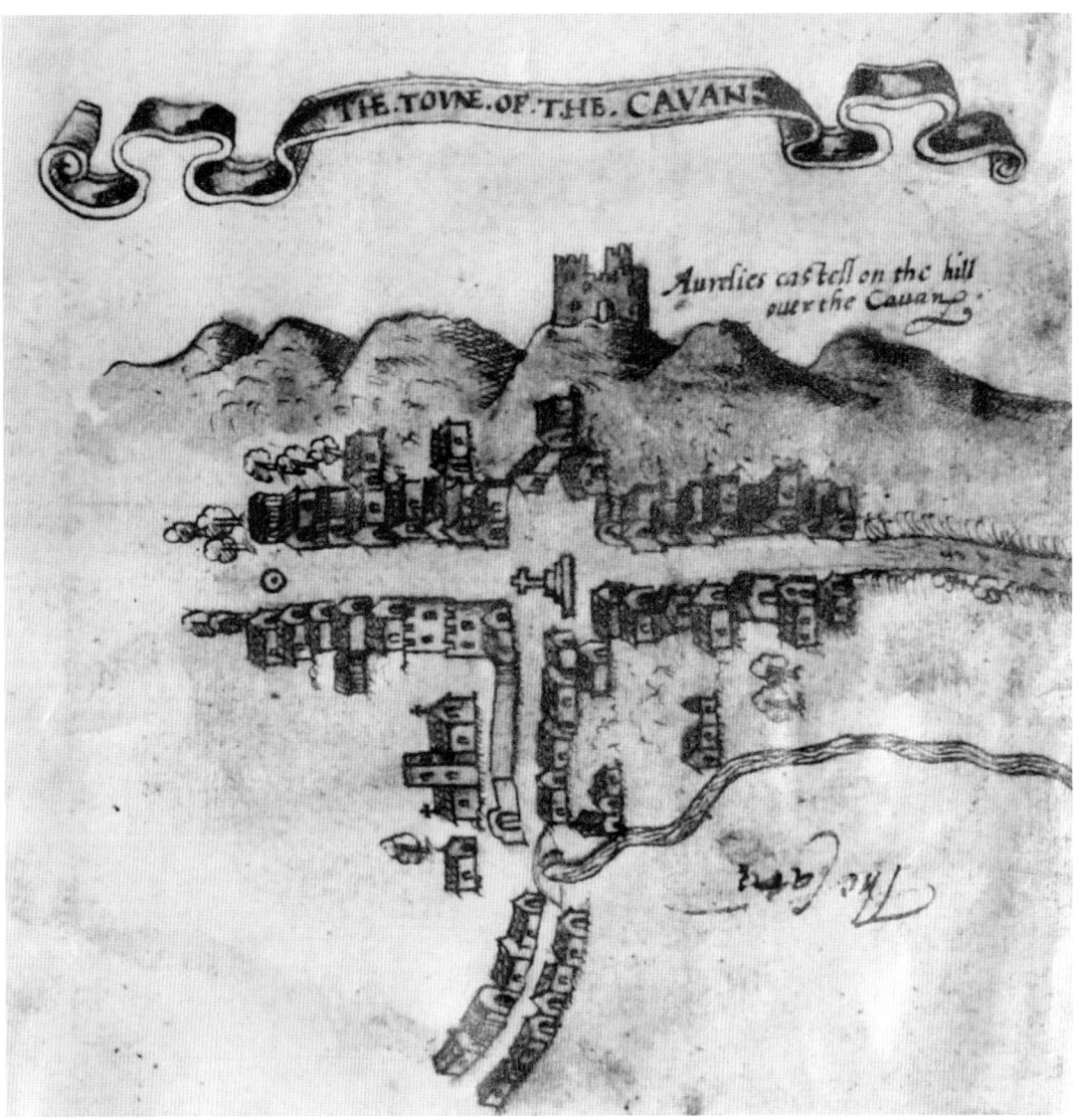

CAVAN

The presence of a well-established settlement and the origins of the modern town are clear from a map of the town in 1591.
Courtesy National Library of Ireland

RELAGH BEG
Relagh Beg
(Twelfth century)

The church, associated with St Fintan of Moybolgue, lies close to a motte and bailey castle. Comprising nave and chancel, the later south transept, which preserves traces of a Tudor window in the gable, doubled for domestic use.

RELAGH BEG

The graveyard contains a rich assembly of small late seventeenth cross fragments as well as a large recumbent slab with a cleric in medieval attire carved in relief.
Courtesy Kevin Mulligan

Cill Mhór ('great church'), underlines an importance that can be traced to the late ninth century. As a fully developed instance of the Romanesque style, it reflects a close engagement between Irish artistic traditions of the twelfth century with those of continental Europe, most likely transmitted along the pilgrimage routes from Rome. The nearest comparison occurs at Clonmacnois with the door to the Nun's Church which, significantly perhaps, was erected in the same period under the patronage of Derbforgaill, wife of Tigernán Ua Ruairc, Queen of Bréifne.

The O'Reillys eventually moved their centre of power from Drumlane to a castle built on an imposing hill at Tullymongan. Below the hill, on a site that would evolve as the modern town of Cavan, Giolla Iosa Ruadh O Raghallaigh founded a Franciscan friary in 1300, retiring there some years later. Afterwards the castle and friary suffered the usual spate of burnings, but a market town continued to develop where the application of commerce and common law was influenced by close interaction with the Pale, especially with Meath; the success of the market had been

(fig.4)
TONYMORE CASTLE
Tonymore
(Sixteenth century)

Defensive features which include a series of neatly dressed stone loops and a murder hole over the entrance indicate the increasingly unsettled state of the country in the Tudor period.
Courtesy Photographic Unit, Dept AHG

enough in 1433 to cause concern, with the Parliament acknowledging that the towns of Meath were losing trade to Cavan.

The castle at Tullymongan survived only until the seventeenth century when sources depicted it as a typical square-plan turreted keep set with an enclosing bawn. Today Tonymore *(fig.4)* represents the only surviving O'Reilly-built stronghold, a stout late sixteenth-century castle south-west of Cavan; only its bulkier proportions distinguish the building from a typical medieval towerhouse. Other contemporary castles survive only as indeterminate ruins. These include Castle Cosby, near Crossdoney, once a substantial structure with two flanking towers of which just a portion of one survives, and the tall ivied keep deep in the woods of Cabra demesne (Dun an Rí) whose identity as an old castle of the Flemings is recalled in the initials 'FF' still to be seen boldly carved onto one of its quoins; this is likely to be the defensive structure shown on the Down Survey in 1656. At Ballymagauran, near Killeshandra, the substantial remains of a rectangular strong house suggests the gradual relaxation of defensive concerns later in the sixteenth century.

The flight of the Earls of Tyrone and Tyrconnell in 1607 cleared the way for a definitive settlement in Ulster, initiated two years later by James I with the plantation of

(fig.5)
BELTURBET
Detail of View of Belturbet by Thomas Roberts, 1770.

Built in 1613, the castle survived intact into the eighteenth century.
Private Collection

Ulster. In order to ensure the stability of the project, Cavan, which only came into being when it was shired in 1579, was one of the six Ulster counties designated for inclusion; in fact Cavan was the first place that Sir Arthur Chichester travelled to in 1610 in order to 'begin that Great work'. As a process of colonisation, the plantation involved the redistribution of estates, primarily those confiscated from exiled earls and their supporters, which were awarded in parcels of between 1,000 and 2,000 acres to 'undertakers' who were obligated to secure their property within two years. This was to be achieved by building a castle in an enclosing bawn and by settling the land with sufficient numbers of loyal subjects from England and Scotland. One of the most imposing of these plantation defences was erected at Belturbet where a large square tower with circular corner turrets *(fig.5)* was built by Sir Stephen Butler to crown the hilltop above an important crossing over the Erne where he had erected a bridge. At Bawnboy, elaborate walls that terminate in a D-shaped enclosure are still to be found in the demesne of the eponymously named

(fig.6)
THE GARDEN HOUSE
Farnham
(Seventeenth century)

Built as a square flanker, and one of four erected at the corners of the bawn, the building on the right was preserved and remodelled in the mid-eighteenth century. Lean-to projections to the side were added with a stair accommodated in one of these leading to the original groin-vaulted room on the first floor.
Courtesy Kevin Mulligan

eighteenth-century house, and it seems likely that these were part of the original bawn erected here by Sir Richard and George Grimes. Nothing is known of Sir Richard Waldron's unfinished plantation castle at Farnham, sold eventually to his carpenter, Richard Castledyne. However one associated seventeenth century remnant is the unusual Garden House *(fig.6)*, a three-storeyed block skewed against the garden wall, close to the Georgian house. This represents a solitary remnant of the bawn built before 1617 by Waldron who was granted 1,000 acres here in 1610.

As a component in the plantation strategy, towns were necessary economically, for the viability of the project, and strategically, to ensure the future stability of the region. They were also considered vital as secure havens, sheltering settlers in an otherwise greatly underdeveloped region with untamed wildernesses of forest and bog. Of the twenty-three new towns proposed throughout the planted counties, many like Cavan, Belturbet and Killeshandra were associated with some kind of existing settlement that also offered specific strategic advantages; Virginia, named for the recently deceased Queen Elizabeth, was, on the other hand, entirely newly conceived, its location half-way between Cavan and Kells also considered strategically convenient. Ballyhaise originated with a typical plantation settlement: in 1610 the Manor of Aghieduff was granted to John Taylor who built a strong bawn of lime and stone above the ford on the Annalee River and introduced a colony of English and Scottish settlers nearby, found to be thriving ten years later with eighteen families living there. Likewise Killeshandra, granted to Sir Alexander Hamilton and his son Claude who planted it with success so that thirty-four 'English-like' houses would eventually be recorded here in 1618. The architectural character of these towns was largely defined by the introduction of English building practices, the widespread appearance of timber 'cage houses' in new formal urban settings representing a remarkable innovation in the region. These innovations however had no lasting impact on native practices, the material proving far too vulnerable during ensuing conflicts.

The plantation settlement provided an opportunity for some new church building, though St Mary's *(fig.7)* in Belturbet, a cruciform building erected soon after 1611, represents the only example that has survived and is still, uniquely, in regular use.

(fig.7)
ST MARY'S CHURCH
Church Street,
Belturbet
(c.1615)

Despite extensive enlargement and internal remodelling in the nineteenth century, the simple architectural character of the original design remains distinct in the fenestration of the main body of the church, where three round-headed lancets are set in a graded composition under a continuous hood-moulding.

(fig.8)
KILMORE OLD CATHEDRAL
Kilmore Upper
(c.1400)

Seat of the Bishops of Kilmore since 1454, the old cathedral, described in 1646 as having a roof of wood and sods, is today a long and rectangular structure that incorporates part of the former palace, represented in the two-storeyed structure over the west end. The Romanesque doorway was removed c.1860 and inserted in the new Church of Ireland cathedral nearby.

Other churches continued in use and were repaired, including the old cathedral at Kilmore *(fig.8)*, which was by far the most important ecclesiastical building; now used as a parish hall it is easily overlooked but the overriding simplicity of a seventeenth-century church interior is preserved in the cambered plaster vault which forms the ceiling and in the primitively carved wooden columns that support the gallery.

(fig.9)
KILLESHANDRA OLD CHURCH
Church Street,
Killeshandra
(1688)

The Renaissance-inspired tracery makes this one of the finest classical churches of the late seventeenth century in Ireland.

(fig.10)
KILLESHANDRA OLD CHURCH

The monumental classical gate piers were erected when the church was remodelled. The date 1688 is inscribed on the frieze, while a small relief panel on each pier displays respectively the crest and arms of Sir Francis Hamilton.

KILLESHANDRA CHURCH OF IRELAND CHURCH

Now located in the town's nineteenth century Church of Ireland church, this bold classical monument erected to Sir Francis Hamilton (d.1713) accords well with the old parish church in which it was originally located. Attributed to David Sheehan, its sumptuous architectural design was possibly inspired by Robert Kidwell's Godfrey monument in Canterbury Cathedral.

Pre 1700

Following the plantation, a deepening polarisation amongst the inhabitants of Ulster became focused on the volatile duality of land and religion that eventually erupted into open rebellion. On 22 October 1641 the Gaelic Irish of Ulster rose up and over the following year succeeded in almost completely destroying the achievements of the plantation in Cavan. At Killeshandra, however, Sir Francis Hamilton had burnt the town himself to prevent it passing into rebel hands. His grandson, another Francis, made amends after the Restoration and had the town rebuilt. Extolled at his death in 1713 as 'an example of integrity in evil times, shining as a steady light', his greatest legacy here remains the parish church *(fig.9)*, in substance a medieval structure but in 1688 remodelled and enlarged by Hamilton to become one of the finest examples of Restoration classicism in Ulster. Hamilton's flamboyant arms are borne proudly on the entrance gable, set between large round-headed windows with distinctive Renaissance-inspired tracery composed with a circle set over two round-headed arches. The gable is held between distinctive piers, buttresses once adorned with urns or finials that reaffirm the overall sense of a guiding baroque classicism that continues with the piers of the entrance gates *(fig.10)*. All this provides an early instance in Cavan of the sophisticated architectural tastes inspired by European classicism that would eventually achieve a full flowering over the course of the following century.

The Eighteenth Century

(fig.11)
FARREN CONNELL
Bobsgrove
(c.1760)

Known in the eighteenth century as Bobsgrove, Farren Connell is a straighforward gable-ended block whose present appearance belies its origins as an important late seventeenth-century house. The massive chimney stacks on the gables give a clue to those origins.

After the Cromwellian and Restoration land settlements the energies and investments of the emergent Protestant ascendancy were concentrated on the accumulation of landed estates which was centred and made most evident with the development of the country house. Farren Connell *(fig.11)*, as one of the earliest undefended country houses built in Cavan, indicates the beginnings of the new era of sustained peace and rising prosperity. With the beginning of the new century the buildings of Cavan continued to provide evidence for this improving situation and the Georgian country house, more than any other building type, provided the principal vehicle for the progress of architectural tastes outside the capital.

Bellamont Forest *(fig.12)* belongs to an important group of early Georgian houses that includes Ballyhaise, Lismore and Cabra, each built by individuals who were members of the Irish Parliament in the same period. This was an affiliation that they shared with Sir Edward Lovett Pearce, the first architect of any consequence or ability in Ireland who designed the new Parliament House in Dublin, a deeply sophisticated building that reaffirmed the power of the classical orders and its place of preference amongst the patrons of the new political order. Pearce's involvement with Bellamont is confirmed by surviving drawings, and it is possible that he had some influence on the design of the others. Built for Thomas Coote, the Palladian spirit of the design is

The Eighteenth Century

(fig.12)
BELLAMONT
Bellamont Forest
(c.1730)

The prominent use of brick perfectly accords with Palladio's own building practices, and here the contrasting effect of the stone detail greatly enhances the architectural power of the building.
Courtesy Irish Architectural Archive

BELLAMONT

The top-lit bedroom lobby at Bellamont is a striking feature of its plan, its influence on the work of Richard Castle evident when it recurs in two later houses, Russborough and Bellinter.
Courtesy Kevin Mulligan

BELLAMONT

Courtesy National Library of Ireland

BELLAMONT

Courtesy Irish Architectural Archive

BELLAMONT

Bellamont and Ballyhaise retain the finest country-house interiors in Cavan, each displaying good examples of the enriched geometric ornament that characterised stucco decoration before 1740. Greatest variety is evident in Bellamont, finest in the flat ceiling of the saloon and in the dining room, shown above, where its high-coved ceiling is enriched by coffers.
Courtesy Irish Architectural Archive

BELLAMONT
Gate lodge

The use of brick reflected an abundance of suitable clay in the district which overcame the difficulties of obtaining suitable building stone.
Courtesy National Library of Ireland

ANNAGHLEE
(1744)

The popularity of brick in this area continued with this attractive early Georgian house which unfortunately no longer survives.
Courtesy Irish Architectural Archive

made explicit in its composition as a freestanding cubic block, a perfect study in proportion and composure that exemplifies the idea of a refined, practical rural retreat at the heart of a landed estate that corresponds precisely with the Italian concept of a villa. The classical inspiration for the design is expressed most overtly in the prostyle Doric portico, the very first monumental temple front to be applied to a domestic building in Ireland. The competent and pleasing way that the contrasting textures of brick and stone were used on Bellamont confirms that the aesthetic and architectural potential of the materials was by then already perfectly well understood; in fact brick enjoyed a particular prominence in this district throughout the eighteenth century as the poor quality of local building stone was overcome by an abundance of suitable clays.

For its pure Palladian form, its compact plan and assured classical detail, Bellamont was to have a profound influence on the development of the Georgian country house, notably in the work of Pearce's assistant, Richard Castle, who was to become the leading country-house architect in Ireland and who is usually named as the architect for Ballyhaise *(fig.13)*, though it is probable that Pearce had a role here also. This property was inherited in 1693 by Colonel Brockhill Newburgh who in the following decades grandly rebuilt his house and established a formally planned village nearby.

(fig.13)
BALLYHAISE HOUSE
Drumcrow
(c.1735)

Built by Brockhill Newburgh and originally composed with wings in the classic Palladian manner (removed when the house was extended in the early nineteenth century), Ballyhaise was deemed by Jonathan Swift, 'not only the best, but the only house he had seen in Ireland'.

BALLYHAISE HOUSE

The close proximity of the house to its agricultural buildings reflected the concept of the Palladian-inspired classical villa as the heart of the working agricultural estate.

(fig.14)
LISMORE CASTLE
Lismore Demesne
(c.1730)

Built for Thomas Nesbitt, Lismore Castle indicates a level of architectural sophistication typical of the work of Sir Edward Lovett Pearce.
Courtesy Irish Architectural Archive

Like Bellamont, the house at Ballyhaise is distinguished as a building predominantly built of brick with its classical detail perfectly mediated, cleanly and precisely, in contrasting stone trim. Instead of a freestanding portico, the idea of the temple front is addressed in the frontispiece, a pedimented breakfront formed with two tiers of pilasters – Ionic over Doric – which observed the strict hierarchy that applies to the classical orders. Ballyhaise was further innovative for its introduction to Irish domestic architecture of the central bowed projection, distinctive here in its accommodation of a complete oval form within the plan, a shape that derives from French baroque architecture of the seventeenth century. Though difficult to conceive now, Ballyhaise was even more remarkable in that its original form had been conceived with the classic expanded Palladian layout, its central block set between curved wings in a manner that enjoyed an enduring popularity in Ireland, having begun with houses like Carton and Castletown in County Kildare. At Ballyhaise, this grand composition with its low arcaded wings terminating in polygonal pavilions, equal to the most ambitious of Palladio's villa designs, was swept away when new wings were formed in the early nineteenth century. The massing of the central block at Ballyhaise between lower square subsidiary towers and a series of small pyramid roofs recurred at

LISMORE CASTLE

Only the wings and one of its subsidiary towers now survive at Lismore.

Lismore *(fig.14)*, where the surviving wings rather more grandly reaffirm the Palladian idea of closely integrating the agricultural practicalities of the farm with the house.

Political stability enhanced the economic potential of the rural economy while the steady development of the physical infrastructure of the county under the grand jury system ensured its success. Comprised of the leading property owners and financed by local taxes which it had the power to levy, each county jury implemented countless road improvements and built new bridges. Reflecting the close and co-operative connections between neighbouring landlords and the mutual advantages a place on the grand jury offered for both county and estate, Brockhill Newburgh and Thomas Nesbitt of Lismore were both overseers for the impressive eight-arch bridge at Ballyhaise *(fig.15)* built to replace the old fording-point on the Annaghlee River. O'Daly's Bridge *(fig.16)* reflects the continuing tradition of bridge-building through the century while its position on the border with County Meath highlights the importance of bridge-building for opening up communication between the regions.

(fig.15)
BALLYHAISE BRIDGE
Drumcrow
(1793)

A formidable structure with angled cutwaters, each extended to accommodate refuges within the parapet; built predominantly of rubble, the dressed coping stones, the simple string course defining the base of the parapet and the cleanly cut arch voussoirs all raise it from a utilitarian structure into a considered work of architecture.

(fig.16)
O'DALY'S BRIDGE
Edenburt
(1762)

A handsomely carved plaque on its parapet bears the date 1762 and displays the bridge name, honouring the owners of the adjoining Blackwater Mills.

The bridge at Ballyhaise was aligned to the advantage of Brockhill Newburgh's house in a way that reinforced the classical formality of the building's original composition. Similar schemes to impose order on the landscape, which were ultimately inspired by French, Dutch and Italian gardening ideas, became a notable characteristic of many early Georgian houses in Cavan including Ballyconnell Castle and Castle Hamilton. Typical features included radiating avenues, canals, parterres and terraces, which still survive to varying degrees at Belville, Farnham, Rathkenny, Red Hills and to good effect around the substantial ruins of the ancient palace at Kilmore *(fig.17)*, a house rebuilt in the early decades of the century and once considered one of the best houses in Ulster, 'fit for a nobleman'. Belville near Bellananagh, a handsome if modest gable-ended Georgian house distinctive for its pronounced ashlar doorcase, was, despite its unassuming scale, once the centre of one of the most ambitious of all these landscapes. Developed by Thomas Fleming, Belville's elaborate water works included a pool before the house, a cascade and a T-shaped canal as well as a banqueting house, which even in ruins remains a prominent hilltop monument known today as Fleming's Folly.

(fig.17)
KILMORE PALACE
Kilmore Upper (c.1720)

A sense of the old formal landscape persists amongst the ruins of the old episcopal palace where in the early eighteenth century Bishop Goodwin levelled and drained a bog and made a canal over 400 metres long, aligned with his front door.
Courtesy Kevin Mulligan

ST PATRICK'S CHURCH
Ballintemple

This elaborate coat of arms of Thomas Fleming, dated 1713, was formerly displayed on the substantial hilltop structure known as Fleming's Folly

(fig.18)
RATHKENNY TEA HOUSE
Dernaskeagh
(c.1730)

Built of plum-coloured brick with rusticated stone quoins, lancet windows and a battlemented parapet, all expressed with a spare elegance, the tea house stands between low quadrant walls to effect an appearance of moderated stateliness.
Courtesy Kevin Mulligan

At Rathkenny, the terraced walled garden is dramatically sited across the river, open on one side to the water and accessed from a footbridge, aligned on the axial central path that terminates at a small Georgian tea house *(fig.18)* on the upper terrace, its adoption of the Gothic style full of the eighteenth-century desire to evoke romanticism in garden buildings and follies. At Red Hills, great pomp attends the prominent classical entrance *(fig.19)* where square stone piers topped by big sculpted pine cones provide an indication of the level of architectural sophistication that could be invested in all elements of the designed landscape. Another notable entrance, formerly associated with Ballyconnell Castle, presents a wide sweep with short ashlar piers, a refined composition that was repeated at Bellville, with each pier decorated with niches and petite crowning urns.

The rising prosperity of the rural economy became increasingly evident in the development of towns and villages in the eighteenth century, many formally planned by local landlords who actively promoted new markets. The role of the grand jury in sponsoring public buildings was made evident in the county town which in the 1740s possessed a county gaol, courthouse and several good inns reflecting the dominant commercial enterprise in most towns. Although the market towns in Cavan continued to evolve steadily so that the urban buildings found in them today are predominately nineteenth century, the general characteristics of the main thoroughfares remain an important legacy of Georgian town planning. In the Ulster tradition, the market square at Belturbet is called the Diamond, and it occupies the upper end of the ascending Butler Street where, until its replacement in the early twentieth century, an imposing Palladian market house of the 1760s was given due prominence on the crest of the rise. A more formal linear plan, common in Ulster since the plantation, was adopted in Bailieborough, the marketplace given prominence as an oblong figure in the centre of the main street. The market house is gone, but on the opposite side the premises of B. O'Reilly dominates, investing the old marketplace with a sense of civic gravitas while upholding the pleasing Georgian character of the original streetscape.

(fig.19)
REDHILLS HOUSE
Redhills
(c.1790)

MARKET STREET
Cootehill

In 1725 Thomas Coote, in his efforts to promote the linen industry throughout the district, obtained a grant for a weekly market and annual fair at Cootehill. This gradually gave the town the impetus to develop along more formal lines with the laying out of Market Street before the end of the century.
Courtesy PJ Dunne Picture Postcard Collection

BALLYHAISE

Before 1730 Brockhill Newburgh conceived an extraordinary circus-like plan for the village of Ballyhaise, laid out as a decagon of which one side with its two-storied houses remains. It formerly enclosed the marketplace, whose centrepiece was a circular market house, long vanished but considered by contemporaries a design considered worthy of 'a Vitruvius or Palladio.'
Courtesy PJ Dunne Picture Postcard Collection

The Eighteenth Century

Handsomely proportioned, three storeys tall, its seven bays are symmetrically composed with traditional shopfronts, rusticated door-surrounds and a central carriage arch.

In the second half of the century Mervyn Pratt ambitiously projected a great broad street at Kingscourt with a pivotal market place in the centre overlooked by the former market house *(fig.20)* which dramatically bridged a perpendicular side street. The steep roofs, stout rubble chimney stacks and primitive rusticated stone doorcases of its largely two-storied buildings all retain an essentially eighteenth-century character, while the Central Stores on the east side represents one of the most attractive formal compositions in Kingscourt with its handsome and reliably solid five-bay front with large twelve-pane sashes and a refined fanlit doorcase to the centre. Several houses with corrugated-iron roofs are a reminder that most of the houses lining the street were thatched until recent times which makes Gartlan's *(fig.21)* premises an exceptional survivor of a straw-thatched building in an urban setting. Unlike the Central Stores, the vernacular qualities of the

(fig.20)
MARKET HOUSE
Kingscourt

Formerly set at the top of the central marketplace, the market house was a relatively informal structure made distinct by its Tudor-Gothic-inspired openings and the gaping central arch that bridged an intersecting side street.
Courtesy PJ Dunne Picture Postcard Collection

(fig.21)
GARTLAN'S
Main Street,
Kingscourt
(c.1780)

This thatched house, which was formerly a post office and later a spirit grocers, represents a rare survival of an urban building in a wholly vernacular tradition.
Courtesy Kevin Mulligan

KING'S COTTAGE
Chapel Road
Bailieborough
(c.1780)

The absence of formal design that characterises vernacular buildings is evident in this modest gable-ended thatched house; its whitewashed rubble walls, miniature twelve-pane sashes and stubby chimney stacks preserve the essential qualities of a once-ubiquitous type of dwelling.

building are evident in its endearing whitewashed front where the haphazard ordering of the fenestration has a pleasing informality, made even more appealing by the wonderfully simple shopfront, placed off centre in a way that is utterly indifferent to the doorway.

The fundamental simplicity which characterises vernacular buildings is due in part to the use of basic natural materials, the creation of modest, practical forms and the application of traditional methods, always the result of the long established practices of local craftsmen responding to the particular conditions of their environment. Thatch continued to represent the most prevalent type of roofing before the nineteenth century. The choice of material varied in each locality determined either by whatever plants were available naturally such as water reed, sedge and heather or from crops, which, depending on agricultural practices, ranged from oat or wheat straw to flax, which was particularly prevalent in the linen districts of Ulster. Throughout the county the basic walling materials were provided by the glacial deposition which created the drumlin landscape, offering an abundance of freely available stone and clay, which could be extracted from the ground with relative ease for building stones, mortars and renders. Though the nature of materials and traditions employed in vernacular buildings can limit the range of architectural potential, individual structures are still capable of displaying great

variety. The buttressed vernacular barn *(fig.22)* by the roadside near Kilnavert is equally arresting for its display of architectural simplicity as for its structural ingenuity. The widespread occurrence of similar buildings attest to the historical tradition of a small farm society in the county, representing the farmsteads of the majority who tenanted no more than five acres, half of which was given over to crops, such as oats, potatoes and in the linen districts to flax, with the remainder as pasturage. Weaving represented an important cottage industry in Ulster during the eighteenth century, reflected in the higher rates of pay earned by weavers: twice those paid to agricultural labourers. The existence of the industry in Cavan, which allowed for the attainment of modest prosperity, might

(fig.22)
BARN
Kilnavert
(c.1800)

The endurance of building traditions and the effortless manner in which buildings were adapted and repaired over centuries means the precise dating of such structures is virtually impossible, but the results invest these buildings with a timeless quality.

account for the improved standard of houses like Rose Cottage *(fig.23)* at Killygowan, located between the lakes of Lough Oughter; here the front elevation adopts an imperfect symmetry, centred on the shallow projection of the entrance as a windbreak.

Higher up the scale, the two-storied house at Knocknalosset *(fig.24)*, built by tenants of the Greville estate, has two contrasting fronts as a perfect marriage of the formal and vernacular traditions in building; to the north, facing into a narrow yard opposite a long lofted barn, a simple four-bay facade where the windows are all sill-less, mostly with miniature Georgian sashes, contrasts dramatically with

(fig.23)
ROSE COTTAGE
Killygowan
(c.1780)

The whitewashed simplicity of the walls is enhanced by the formality of its well-proportioned sashes – each window setting six panes over three.

(fig.24)
KNOCKNALOSSET HOUSE
Knocknalosset
(c.1780)

Inside, the plan is laid out with five low-ceilinged, lime-washed rooms on the ground floor, arranged around a long hall incorporating a narrow stairs. The kitchen wall at the centre has the usual generously arched hearth while a feature that was just as essential to its occupants is the squint opening through the stair wall, a necessary window on passing life.

KNOCKNALOSSET HOUSE
Rear elevation

The Eighteenth Century

the formal three-bay south façade, refenestrated in the late Georgian period when it was given enlarged openings with tripartite sashes and sandstone sills. Only matters of scale and a stricter observance of symmetry seem to separate Rose Cottage from the handsomely modest gentleman's villa at Ricehill *(fig.25)*, a neat gable-ended block with a single storey front concealing a basement and attic with twelve-pane Georgian sashes and central doorway, flanked by narrow fanlights.

(fig.25)
RICEHILL
Coolnagor or Ricehill
(c.1760)

The tripartite arrangement of the entrance was based on the Venetian or Palladian window which enjoyed continuing popularity in later Georgian architecture.

CAVAN ABBEY
Abbey Street,
Cavan
(c.1460)

The tall square tower, all that remains of the seventeenth-century parish church in Cavan, has a series of round-headed openings to the belfry each, like the doorway, expressed in a bold 'Gibbsian' manner with blocked surrounds as part of remodelling works in about 1750.

(fig.26)
DRUMLOMAN CHURCH
Bracklagh
(1739)

A weather-worn plaque on the west gable informs that 'This church was built at the expense of William Gore of Woodford, Esq. in the year 1739'.

The established church entered the eighteenth century in a poor state after the affrays of the previous century. Parish churches had become neglected, either badly decayed or ruined, as church property, including tithes, had passed into lay hands leaving an inadequate number of clergy very poorly supported financially while attendance at public worship was equally deficient. Although few churches were built in the first half of the century, the now derelict little church at Drumloman *(fig.26)* is a notable exception. It is an austerely simple single cell of three bays, plainly rendered without any architectural pretension whatsoever and only made Gothic when new windows were inserted a century later. Where the opportunity to renew or build parish churches arose an abiding architectural preference for classicism prevailed. Still in use, Tomregan parish church *(fig.27)* at Ballyconnell is a classical building of rare sophistication, built in 1757 under the patronage of the landlord George Leslie Montgomery. Small, but grand in concept, its

(fig.27)
TOMREGAN CHURCH
Doon
(1756)

Enlarged and refenestrated to Gothic tastes in the early nineteenth century, which included the addition of a tower and spire, it still retains its carved doorcase – a bold classical design with a characteristically eighteenth-century lugged architrave and a more unusual shaped pediment.

TOMREGAN CHURCH

Inside the surviving eighteenth-century plasterwork is equally classical and bold, typical of the period but of a quality and extent rarely found in such a provincial context at this time.

(fig.28)
HOLY TRINITY CHURCH
Kildoagh
(1796)

Built for the Revd Patrick Maguire as a long thatched hall of five bays, enlarged in 1860, and now disused, this remains an important instance of a vernacular church building.
Courtesy Irish Architectural Archive

plan is particularly striking, an unconventional cruciform shape with bowed ends.

The discriminatory measures instituted against Catholics from the end of the seventeenth century, although ineffective in discouraging widespread continuance of religious practices, impacted on church building which for most of the century were represented by unassuming vernacular structures. Even as relief measures were introduced in 1782, restrictions on the exercise of religion continued, specifically in the measure that 'no chapel can have a steeple or bell'. Holy Trinity, Kildoagh *(fig.28)*, though a rather late building of 1796, in complying with these restrictions perfectly embodied the conventions of the rural 'mass-house' that existed during the century. Still retaining its clay floor tiles, the interior was laid out with the altar placed in the centre of the long south wall, a common arrangement with simple bench pews set in rows opposite and, at each

HOLY TRINITY CHURCH

The interior retains its clay floor tiles, and the windows their busy display of the linear Y-tracery that typifies the charming naiveties of Georgian 'Gothick'.
Courtesy Irish Architectural Archive

end, opposing galleries. Kildoagh represents an even greater rarity given that full emancipation in the nineteenth century provided the widespread incentive to rebuild.

The immigration of Scottish settlers to Ulster as part of the Ulster plantation accounts for the high proportion of Presbyterian churches in Cavan; largely composed of tenant farmers like their Catholic counterparts, the modest means of the congregations is reflected in the unassuming character of their meeting-houses.

CROAGHAN PRESBYTERIAN CHURCH
Coolnashinny or Croaghan (1742)

There is nothing overtly architectural to distinguish this modest building, a hall four bays deep, simply gabled to the front. The gable apex carries a finial with the date 1742.

The Eighteenth Century

CORGLASS PRESBYTERIAN CHURCH
Lisgar
(1795)

A large seven-bay hall built by the Rev Montgomery that was originally thatched with attractive Gothick windows, its architectural character was shared by other vernacular churches, including the contemporary chapel at Kildoagh.
Courtesy Leslie McKeague

CORGLASS PRESBYTERIAN CHURCH
The attractive and pleasing simplicity continues inside where Georgian box pews with raised and fielded panelling remain, along with a raking gallery that extends the length of the hall, carried on iron columns.

FARNHAM STREET
Cavan
(c.1820)

These early nineteenth-century terraces carry over the basic qualities of Georgian design in the use of handsome proportions. The integrated archways lead to substantial mews buildings set to the rear.
Courtesy Kevin Mulligan

ERSKINE TERRACE
Cavan
(c.1860)

The raised basements make the elevations more imposing, elevating the entrance above the street with a grand flight of steps.
Courtesy Kevin Mulligan

The Nineteenth Century

As agricultural exports continued to rise in the early decades of the nineteenth century, buoyed by the wars against Napoleon, thriving provincial markets ensured that the primary focus of building activity was concentrated in towns. The military successes in Europe were celebrated on a plaque on the market house at Ballyjamesduff, designed by the Cavan-born architect Arthur McClean and built in 1813, 'a year memorable for the Glorious achievements of Marquis Wellington'. This commanding block presides over an expansive marketplace, its design modestly classical with a carefully ordered five-bay front where the circular, or oeil-de-boeuf windows, recessed on the first floor, form a distinguishing element of the design that was to be repeated in 1821 at Bellananagh. The three-bay rubble building at Bailieborough however, with its pedimented frontispiece and boldly expressed arches, is a more typical example of the market houses built throughout Ireland at this time, a type that also once existed in Cavan and Cootehill.

In each instance these buildings reflected the continuing influence of landlords on urban development, whose active proprietorial interest frequently set the tone for fashionable improvements. At Virginia, the expansion of the village into an attractive estate town was orchestrated by the Marquess of Headfort, while in Cavan Lord Farnham projected a new street, named in his honour, as a generous straight thoroughfare contrasting with the lazy meander of the adjoining Main Street. It soon acquired three-storied late Georgian terraces on

16 FARNHAM STREET
Cavan
(c.1820)

This house is set in the middle of one of the earliest terraces on Farnham Street, an example of a residence built for the professional classes. Percy French, the artist, entertainer and civil engineer lived in this house from 1881 while employed as inspector of drains in Cavan.

AN INTRODUCTION TO THE ARCHITECTURAL HERITAGE of COUNTY CAVAN

DISTILLERY HOUSE
Mill Walk
Belturbet
(1825)

A distillery established by Messrs. Dickson, Dunlop & Co. became a thriving industry that was capable of producing 100,000 gallons of whiskey annually. Long closed, its existence is still represented by an attractive late-Georgian residence, a long block distinguished by its charming doorway with its pretty leaded fanlight.

(fig.29)
DRUMHILLAGH MILL
Drumhillagh
(c.1820)

Despite their scale, these substantial rubble mills have an unassuming quality that allows them to integrate well with the rural environment in a way that reflects an abiding characteristic of nineteenth-century industrial architecture.

the east side whose tall proportions and carefully ordered sash windows, pretty fanlit doorcases and railed front gardens gave the street a gentrified air; this reflected contemporary concerns with matters of social propriety by separating the businesses and residences of the professions, then on the rise, from the less salubrious and busy commerical core.

Like most Ulster towns, markets for cattle and linen were key pillars of trade within the rural economy, though the linen industry would decline considerably in Cavan over the course of the century as other industrial centres in the north expanded. In the countryside where mixed farming represented the central rural occupation, flour-milling was a vital ancillary industry and the simple vernacular character of the buildings typically connected with it are well represented by the large rubble buildings at Drumhillagh *(fig.29)*. These, even though long disused, remain perfectly evocative of hard-won harvests and the slow and satisfying processes associated with grinding corn. That process still endures at the Lifeforce Mill *(fig.30)*, a much-enlarged complex of vernacular buildings in the centre of Cavan town, where milling on the Cavan River has been established for many centuries.

The abolition of the Irish legislature in 1800

(fig.30)
LIFEFORCE MILL
River Street,
Cavan
(c.1870)

Greatly enlarged between 1990 and 1995, and partly constructed using fabric from a disused nineteenth-century mill brought from Drogheda, this mill retains the simple vernacular character that was typical of many nineteenth-century industrial buildings. Inside, the machinery is powered by a MacAdam water turbine of 1846.

brought considerable renewal within the county, partly to ensure the stability of the Union, as funds distributed to grand jurys were expended on a major building programme that included courthouses and gaols. The erection of Cavan courthouse *(fig.31)* on Farnham Street in 1824 to a fitting neo-classical design asserted a pivotal civic authority at the centre of the new street that it still maintains today. Designed by William Farrell and built in biscuit-coloured sandstone ashlar, quarried locally at Latt, its broad front of five bays offers

(fig.31)
CAVAN COURTHOUSE
Farnham Street,
Cavan
(1824)

The position of the building, set well back from the street in a railed court, asserts its civic authority.

COOTEHILL COURTHOUSE
Market Street,
Cootehill
(1833)

Sometimes attributed to William Deane Butler, its underlying classicism is referenced by the use of pediments over the central bay and on the finely composed stone doorcase. The design was later repeated at Ballyconnell given greater formality by the addition of a portico.

(fig.32)
LURGAN CHURCH
Main Street,
Virginia
(1821)

The designer was Arthur McClean, a Cavan-born architect who had earlier designed the Market House in Ballyjamesduff before he emigrated to Canada in 1825 where he designed further buildings for the Anglican church. A notable feature of the building is the use of cast-iron crockets on the pinnacles.

MULLAGH CHURCH
Mullagh
(1829)

Mullagh church is a perfect example of its type, and such was its popularity that even when the old church at Kildallon was remodelled with a new tower in 1815, Bowden reoriented its configuration to suit the standard design.

a pleasing display of surface recession while the thick-set pilasters on the corners help to assert the seriousness of its function. Bailieborough, built 1818, is altogether more vernacular, a solid smooth-rendered block remarkable principally for its cubic porch, nicely articulated with an inset doorcase framed by slender pilasters with console brackets.

At Cootehill and Virginia, the parish churches were made the primary focus of urban improvements. Lurgan parish church *(fig.32)* in Virginia is set in the large island formed by two important approaches to the town that converge on Main Street. The scenic framing of the battlemented east end, with its traceried window and signal spire, underlines the picturesque potential of the Gothic style. In designing this church Arthur McClean adopted the hall and tower type which became favoured for parish churches from the late eighteenth century as part of the expanding building campaigns of the Board of First Fruits. Although the board employed its own architects, designers like McClean were also introduced by local vestries, probably through the influence of landlords, to achieve works of

(fig.33)
ST JOSEPH'S CHURCH
Corlea
(c.1840)

greater ambition. Amongst the most accomplished is Urney parish church on Farnham Street, a building on which the board's architect, John Bowden, seems to have collaborated with another, tentatively identified as Richard Elsam. The careful massing of the composition marks it out for attention, achieved in a series of diminishing projections from which the tower and spire rise to share in a lively display of bristling Gothic ornament provided by battlements, angle buttresses and crocketted pinnacles. Inside, a continuous timber gallery surrounds the nave under the elegant plaster rib vaults. For the most part however the standard church design was only nominally Gothic, built of rubble and roughcast with dressed-stone details, which Bowden endorsed for most of the new

ST ANNE'S CHURCH
Virginia Road,
Bailieborough
(1838)

St Anne's began as a modest T-plan building which only later developed a greater architectural sophistication, initially with the addition of a tower in 1854, and a chancel in 1869 making the plan wholly cruciform. All these later works were attended by elaborate Gothic enrichment.

churches designed between 1814 and his death in 1822.

The surviving façade of the early nineteenth-century church at Kingscourt, a tall and rugged Gothic gable with battlements, held between square pinnacled towers, overlooks the town as a proud edifice that anticipated the resurgence of the Catholic Church following the achievement of full emancipation in 1829. However St Ultan's, Killinkere, built in the year of emancipation, reflects the continuing tradition for unadorned roughcast buildings with low slate roofs, only made obviously ecclesiastical by the cross raised over the gable and by the generous provision of large pointed windows; invariably, as in the preceding century, these were given timber Y-tracery, which can still be seen to good effect on St Joseph's church *(fig.33)* in Corlea, built about 1836.

William Farrell assumed responsibility for the continuing building activities of the Board of First Fruits in Ulster after Bowden's death, and by 1830 introduced a neatly contained single-cell design for smaller parish churches and chapels of ease. The basic design, applied with minor variations at Larah, Munterconnaught (both 1832), Derrylane (1833) and Dernakesh (1834), was devised as a simple gable-fronted hall inspired by the perpendicular Gothic style, with slender lancets, pinnacled polygonal buttresses to the corners, a striking bell-cote in dressed stone to the main gable and sometimes, as at Munterconnaught *(fig.34)*, with a battlemented entrance porch.

(fig.34)
MUNTERCONNAUGHT CHURCH
Knockatemple
(1831)

The design follows a standard form used throughout the county. This example is amongst the most highly finished, as is evident from its ashlared west front and battlemented porch.

MUNTERCONNAUGHT CHURCH

The striking pierced cast-iron roof trusses are a typical feature in most of William Farrell's smaller churches. A hard brittle alloy of iron that became widely used as result of the industrial revolution, the strength of the material under compression and its decorative potential are well demonstrated here.

Scaled up, the same design was used for Killeshandra (1838) and again with the addition of a tower at Ballyjamesduff (1834) and Bailieborough, where the tower was clearly necessary for so prominent an urban context. Modest gable-fronted halls were preferred amongst the smaller Protestant congregations. The Methodist churches at Ballyjamesduff, Blacklion (1849) and Ballyconnell (1869) are all relatively unadorned buildings with lancets, in accordance with their religious tradition, while the Scots Presbyterian church *(fig.35)* at Cavan of 1836 is, by contrast, a perfectly polished architectural delight.

The Nineteenth Century

KILLESHANDRA CHURCH
Portaliff Glebe
(1842)

Courtesy Representative Church Body

(fig.35)
CAVAN PRESBYTERIAN CHURCH
Farnham Street,
Cavan
(1836)

Designed on a diminutive scale, it is a Tudor-style hall with a battlemented porch, built in squared limestone with sandstone dressings and attractive finials on its gables.

VIEW OF COOTEHILL BY W. GROVES C.1835.

The impressive spired Church of Ireland church with its busy silhouette of pinnacles and battlements was placed dramatically at the east end of Market Street, while the more modest Catholic chapel asserts itself on a side street as a simple gabled hall, its particular denomination identified by the cross-topped-bell-cote.
Courtesy Royal Irish Academy

St Patrick's, Shercock, built in 1838, also attests to the popularity for gable-fronted halls amongst Catholic churches, with one of the most refined examples found integrated within the streetscape in Virginia – a fully blown buttressed Gothic façade in ashlared limestone, built in 1845. Ballyconnell *(fig.36)*, which replaced a nondescript thatched building in 1843, also employs squared limestone to achieve a trim, highly finished hall of three bays with a competent Gothic character evident in the use of narrow lancets and in the kneelered gable which was given a Tudor-style arch to the doorway.

(fig. 36)
OLD CHURCH
Ballyconnell
(1843)

The large arches that surround the eastern bay on each side of the nave are a telling provision for the future expansion of the church, allowing for the addition of transepts to accommodate an increased congregation. Almost certainly the devastating consequences of the Great Famine destroyed that potential.

ST MARY'S CHURCH
Kilconny
(1845-53)

Prominently sited in open countryside, the vigorous treatment of the gable front with expensively carved Gothic detail reflects the growing assertiveness of the Catholic Church. Its bulky proportions indicate a growing population, which would soon be decimated by famine and emigration.

The Nineteenth Century

KNIPE MAUSOLEUM
Widow's House Lane
Belturbet
(c.1850)

Its modest cubic form is enriched by the treatment of its ashlar front, given a horned pediment and an Egyptian-style tapering doorcase, devices associated with the early nineteenth-century interest in the Greek revival.

PHILIP SMITH MEMORIAL
St Felim's Church
Ballinagh
(1894)

This fluted Doric column in granite, erected as a memorial to members of the Smith family of Kevitt Castle, represents a pure exercise in Greek classicism; its design is made more striking by the architectural incongruity of the cross placed on the pedestal.

(fig.37)
FARNHAM HOUSE
Farnham
(1802)

With interiors of c.1790 designed for the first earl of Farnham by the foremost English neo classical architect, James Wyatt, the building was doubled in size in 1802 for the second earl by Francis Johnston who chose to pay tribute to Wyatt's refined approach to detail. His works here now stand alone, retained after Wyatt's interiors were swept away in 1961.
Courtesy Irish Architectural Archive

Whereas a preference for the Gothic style amongst all religious denominations was largely tied to function, evoking a spiritual aptness inspired by medieval precedents, the competing preference between classical and Gothic styles for larger country houses usually reflected the personal taste of the patron. At Farnham *(fig.37)*, a house which had been modelled several times over the eighteenth century, classicism continued to prevail when Francis Johnston greatly enlarged the house in 1802, designing a Doric portico based on the primitive baseless order associated with temples from the fifth century BC. It represents a notable instance of pure Greek revival resulting from the growing awareness of archaeological discoveries in Greece and Italy. Although, like most of his contemporaries, Johnston was an equally proficient master of the Gothic style, the rest of his work in Cavan adopted a chaste form of classicism. This was first evident in his remodelling of Cloverhill House in 1799, and was still clear in his design for the Royal School in Cavan of 1819.

The Nineteenth Century

FARNHAM HOUSE

The pure Greek-inspired form of the portico, whose columns were retained when the house was rationalised in 1961, reflects the greater understanding and appreciation of classical architecture that resulted from improved travel opportunities and the growth in architectural publications since the late eighteenth century.

FARNHAM HOUSE

Francis Johnston's elegant cantilevered staircase with its oval plan and delicate neo classical details was designed to complement the late eighteenth-century interiors in the house by James Wyatt. These no longer survive.

63

FARNHAM SCHOOL, FARNHAM STREET
Farnham Street
(c.1800)

Still in use as a school, the building adopts a distinctly domestic appearance, representing a work of quiet classical sophistication that is usually attributed to Francis Johnston. The use of shallow recesses, into which windows of the wings are set, is of a trademark of his work and recurs in the Cavan Royal School, which he designed in 1819.

MILL VALE
Cornagarrow
(c.1850)

A modest miller's house with walls built of sufficiently good-quality masonry for the stone to remain exposed, contrasted with brick for the reveals, while the doorcase with its tall proportions is finely executed in a pale sandstone.

The Nineteenth Century

(fig. 38)
KILDALLON GLEBE
Bocade Glebe
(1821)

The main facade presents an especially pleasing variant of the typical three-bay design; the basement is concealed on the main front, and a two-storey canted bay with larger, tripartite windows breaks forward on one side.

(fig. 40)
TEMPLEPORT HOUSE
Port
(c.1860)

The well-ordered farm buildings are essentially vernacular in character and constitute an integral ensemble associated with a handsomely composed late-Georgian farmhouse, built for a properous farmer.

(fig. 39)
KILLINAGH GLEBE
Termon
(1827)

Its compact cubic form and roughcast walls enhance the pleasing simplicity of the façade; the carefully differentiated window proportions and the setting of the handsome fanlit doorcase in an arched recess are characteristic of enduring neo classical tastes.

A similar character was preferred amongst middle-sized houses, most designed as a compact two-storey block, with or without a basement, either roughcast or smooth-rendered and with all the architectural emphasis reserved for the main front, given three bays with pleasing window proportions and a central doorcase, often fanlit as in earlier Georgian examples. Rectories represent one of the most prevalent examples of the type, with the glebe houses of Killinagh *(fig.38)* and Kildallon *(fig.39)* amongst those built in the early decades of the century in Cavan, while houses of the minor gentry and prosperous farmers are represented respectively by Tullyvin House and Templeport House *(fig.40)*.

65

An Introduction to the Architectural Heritage of County Cavan

FARNHAM HOUSE BRIDGE
Farnham
(c.1800)

Watercolour, c.1810, by C.B. Wynne from Farnham Album
Built to carry the public road over the main avenue, the relationship between buildings and landscape was enhanced in the nineteenth century by ideas of the picturesque. The Gothic style was central to those ideas and enhances the picturesque qualities of the bridge.
Courtesy Lady Farnham

The enthusiasm for revived historic styles in country-house design was partly fuelled by favourable economic conditions on landed estates, which encouraged greater architectural ambitions. At Kingscourt, Cabra Castle *(fig.41)* is a vigorously massed medievalising fantasy that evolved in two principal building phases, beginning in 1808 when Henry Foster remodelled an existing structure, adopting rather tame, superficial Gothic devices that did little to conceal the character and proportion of the underlying Georgian house. The intended drama and romance of the effect was greatly improved after Joseph Pratt acquired the castle in 1813. He enlarged it considerably, introducing more variety and interest by using a greater panoply of Gothic detail, including turrets and mullioned windows, to achieve a

(fig.41)
CABRA CASTLE
Cormey
(c.1810)

The different phases of the building were successfully integrated under continuous crenellations and a unifying palette of roughcast render and stone dressings. The turreted entrance tower forms a tall and forbidding structure which stands forward at the end of the main wing.

CABRA CASTLE

In contrast to the Gothic power of its exterior, the interiors at Cabra Castle are decorated in a more restrained but equally pleasing way.

CABRA CASTLE

Composed of cast-iron, fanciful square piers enriched by pierced Gothic tracery and crowning crocketted pinnacles frame the railed sweeps that form an embrace on either side of the entrance.

more convincing, picturesque ensemble. In the north of the county, Castle Saunderson *(fig.42)* represents another equally ambitious remodelling of the same period, effected when the large classical house was rigorously draped in more cumbersome Gothic finery. The entrance tower with polygonal corner turrets was inspired by the great English Elizabethan house of Burghley, and placed in the centre of the main front, in a way that reinforced the symmetry of the old house, whereas the adjoining south front was given greater variety, expressed with Tudor gables and made fully asymmetrical by a lower service wing at right angles that continues into an arcaded orangery.

Established as a characteristic of regency houses, bowed projections were favoured on the houses designed by William Farrell, given a shallow profile where otherwise a more robust form of classicism is evident, marking the advent of the Victorian tastes for generally bolder, and richer details. Farrell's designs for Rathkenny and the See House *(fig.43)* at Kilmore are closely similar and share his

(fig.42)
CASTLE SAUNDERSON
Castle Saunderson Demesne
(c.1835)

Conceived by George Sudden, its details, largely executed in rock-faced masonry, were directly inspired by the rugged muscularity of the nearby Crom Castle in Fermanagh, completed just a few years before.
Courtesy National Library of Ireland

CASTLE SAUNDERSON CHURCH
Castle Saunderson Demesne
(c.1835)

George Sudden adopted the same rugged character for the small estate church which adds greatly to the picturesque qualities of the demesne, an exceptional natural landscape on the edge of the Erne system, its attractiveness enhanced by magnificent oaks.

(fig.43)
KILMORE SEE HOUSE
Kilmore Upper
(1835-7)

Inside, both Rathkenny and Kilmore See House share Farrell's preference for giving a central prominence to the stairhall within the plan, surrounded by generously proportioned rooms with enriched plaster cornices and foliated centrepieces.
Courtesy National Library of Ireland

interest in giving strong vertical emphasis to his facades, especially on the corners, while the elaborate treatment around windows with bracketed pilasters and entablatures, notably around the tripartite openings, is a distinct trademark.

Kilnacrott *(fig.44)*, built for Pierce Morton, represented a curious mix of Tudor Gothic and neo-classicism, with interiors richly decorated to early Victorian tastes. The building was greatly reduced in scale in 1880 leaving the Tudor-styled main block and its contiguous yard. Set to one side, the limestone portico is conceived as monument in its own right, deeply projected to receive carriages as a porte cochère with tall, delightful proportions that give it a slender elegance that recalls the work of Regency architects John Nash and Humphrey Repton. Both of these architects

CORRAVAHAN
Corravahan
(1821)

Built as a rectory for Drung parish, and designed by William Farrell, its tall proportions and rather sober expression are pleasantly countered by the offset placement of the bay window and of the full-height bow, a favoured device of the architect, on the adjoining main façades.

(fig.44)
KILNACROTT HOUSE
Kilnacrott
(c.1845)

The façade is made deliberately asymmetrical by an oriel window on one side and an exceptionally fine porte cochère. Built of limestone ashlar with tall, attenuated proportions, the polygonal turrets rising into battlemented crowns add elegance the structure.
Courtesy National Library of Ireland

(fig.45)
KILLYKEEN COTTAGE
Killykeen
(1819)

Originally given a straw thatched roof, its design exploited the natural and rustic qualities of the vernacular tradition while adopting a formal plan where two contrasting symmetrical fronts employed rustic columns fashioned from tree trunks.
Courtesy National Library of Ireland

promoted romantic ideals in architecture which, partly inspired by contemporary works of art and literature, found its perfect embodiment in rustic garden buildings such as the cottage orné. An important example *(fig.45)*, built on what was then part of the Farnham estate, survives in Killykeen Forest Park, sited near the water's edge on a peninsula in Lough Oughter.

The picturesque qualities of the cottage orné were successfully distilled into a simpler style of architecture for the gate lodges at Virginia where the Marquess of Headfort employed the garden designer and architect Alexander McLeish in the 1820s to develop a sporting estate on the shore of Lough Ramor, and to embellish the village with several new buildings, all in the same taste. Though generally restrained, the features which distinguish these buildings include polygonal brick chimney stacks, cross-mullioned or quarry-glazed windows and decorative bargeboards.

PARK HOTEL/VIRGINIA LODGE
Virginia

Built as a sporting lodge by the Marquess of Headfort and later occupied as a dower house, its design in a cottage style was fitting for its picturesque setting.

ESTATE HOUSES
Virginia
(c.1820)

These attractive mid-nineteenth century estate houses have open porches on which the rustic timber supports have been modelled in cast iron.
Courtesy Kevin Mulligan

PARK HOTEL/VIRGINIA LODGE
Ballyjamesduff Road,
Virginia
(c.1820)

This lodge, attributed to Alexander McLeish, is one of several buildings around the estate designed in a picturesque cottage style.

The Nineteenth Century

(fig.46)
PORTLONGFIELD SCHOOL
Portlongfield
(c.1830)

An especially well-preserved example of several schoolhouses built in the 1820s by Lord Farnham to promote the 'moral and religious character and improvement of the tenantry', a key principle of his method of estate management.

DRUMCOGHILL CHURCH HALL
Drumcoghill
(c.1820)

Built as a school, deep in the countryside, this building is an unexpected delight, transformed by the extraordinary design of its cast-iron casement windows, a flamboyant display of Gothic tracery that is sensationally brought alive by swirling dagger motifs.

A similar restraint, tending firmly towards the vernacular, is also found in the schools built in the same period at Kiffagh, Derrylane and Port Longfield *(fig.46)*, all unadorned roughcast blocks in which the use of twin quarry-glazed casements divided by a central mullion represents a feature borrowed from the cottage style.

As the provision of welfare became a matter of increasing public concern in the nineteenth century, the government acted to relieve the human destitution by introducing the Irish Poor Law Act of 1838 which established elected Boards of Guardians to implement the workhouse system. The local Board oversaw the erection of buildings to a standard plan devised by George Wilkinson as architect to the Poor Law Commissioners. The well-preserved example at Cavan, built in 1841, represents the earliest group, designed with gables in an understated Tudor idiom that was popular amongst other contemporary institutional buildings. Here the two-storied administrative block, with its five-bay symmetrical front of good quality squared limestone, stands to the fore, and was originally where destitute families were received before admission into the more austere series of accommodation ranges formally laid out behind. When Bawnboy workhouse was built in 1851 Wilkinson greatly

ST FELIM'S HOSPITAL
Cavan
(1847)

Part of the complex associated with Cavan workhouse, this former fever hospital is a sober work with rudimentary Tudor detail, yet it remains an imposing structure of considerable quality and interest.

(fig.47)
SANDY ROW
Farnham
(c.1830)

Lord Farnham recommended that the smallest houses, those of cottiers, should contain three apartments, with a glazed window in each – and the houses should be whitewashed every year, inside and out.

altered his conventional design, inverting his plan and adopting a simpler, vernacular character comprising long, unadorned roughcast ranges with attractive quarry-glazed windows – somewhat incongruous elements of the cottage style that were nonetheless successfully adapted for a complex on such an impressive scale.

A response to the moral obligation to improve basic living conditions amongst an increasingly impoverished tenant population was also demonstrated by landlords who promoted building improvements on their estates. While ostensibly motivated by a desire to enhance the moral and social welfare of society, such actions were also concerned with addressing the unsustainable problem of a rapidly expanding population which undermined the viability of estates. Lord Farnham devised six plans ranging 'from the thatched cottage of the cottier to the slated farm-house of two stories high' in order to encourage farmers to build new homes and further incentivised his tenants with an offer to pay half the cost for the slate and foreign timber on new houses. The estate cottages at Sandy Row *(fig.47)* represent perfect models of the improved housing advocated by Farnham, a neat group of four lofted houses, each with its individual garden. Other examples, built in the same spirit, include the pair of roadside cottages at Redhills, both enhanced by deep layers of whitewash and small square sashes. More substantial farmhouses were also

(fig.48)
HOUSE
Behernagh
(c.1800)

A satisfyingly solid structure, rising well above the ordinary with a pleasing three-bay front and sash windows, all handsomely proportioned around a pretty fanlit doorcase in the centre.

MOUNTAIN VIEW
Kilsallagh
(1881)

As a small rural farmstead, the formal character and quality of the design displayed in the house is somewhat unexpected and forms an interesting contrast to the charming group of vernacular yard buildings with which it is intimately associated.

advocated and several examples were built by tenants of the Headfort estate, best demonstrated in the exceptionally well-preserved farm at Behernagh *(fig.48)*. Behind the house, the simple vernacular farm buildings all remain intact, forming an orderly and deeply attractive group around a cobbled yard, all corresponding to Lord Farnham's advice that byers, barns and dunghills should be kept to the rear, leaving the front to stand neat and clean as a model of wellbeing and prosperity, the rewards of honest industry.

The Gothic revival became the transforming architectural movement of the nineteenth century as its adherents encouraged ecclesiastical architects to follow with greater faithfulness the lessons of medieval Gothic design. Buildings became texturally richer as exposed masonry became popular with walling frequently blended coarse or quarry-faced masonry with smooth dressings; architectural profiles become more faithful to medieval models while, generally, carved detail increased, becoming richer and more naturalistic. While the dominant figure was A.W.N Pugin, another important exponent was the London architect William Slater whose St Feidhlimidh's Cathedral *(fig.49)* represents the most important Gothic-revival building in the county. Built in a blend of local limestone and pale Dungannon sandstone, it successfully introduces the late medieval phase of Gothic architecture known as the Decorated style which is displayed prominently here in the use of rich geometric tracery. Inside, a tall arcaded nave with compound piers opening into the aisles is roofed in dark unpainted timber. The careful ornamentation of the space, avoiding unnecessary decoration, serves largely to convey the intrinsic virtues of the different materials used, and accords with Pugin's deeply held views on the appropriate decoration of buildings.

(fig.49)
ST FEIDHLIMIDH'S CATHEDRAL
Kilmore Upper

A tightly massed cruciform structure, ascending to a squat crossing tower, it stands impressively and evocatively in its ancient rural setting outside Cavan town.

AN INTRODUCTION TO THE ARCHITECTURAL HERITAGE *of* COUNTY CAVAN

ST FEIDHLIMIDH'S CATHEDRAL
Courtesy National Library of Ireland

The Nineteenth Century

Completed in 1860, St Feidhlimidh's Cathedral was built by the Cavan contractor William Hague, whose builders' yard was based on Market Street in the town. He was employed extensively on church commissions, including the churches at Quivvy and Cloverhill, and it is perhaps not surprising therefore that his son, also William, should become one of the foremost exponents of the Gothic revival. The younger Hague was the major ecclesiastical architect for the resurgent Catholic Church in the second half of the nineteenth century, though his earliest work is represented by the former Weslyan church on Farnham Street, a decidedly competent Gothic design of 1858 which proudly carried an offset broach spire, since removed. It was built soon after his return to Ireland following a period in the London office of the great Victorian architect Sir Charles Barry, partner with Pugin on the Westminster Houses of Parliament. The extent to which Hague absorbed fully the central tenets of the Gothic revival is best represented by the delightful small village church of St Aidan *(fig.50)* at Butler's Bridge, built with his father as contractor - as he continued to be on many of his son's succeeding projects in the county. Striking for its jaunty offset spirelet, St Aidan's displays a use of diverse materials that distinguishes the architect's work; banded masonry, deployed in an attractive, measured way perfectly demonstrates all the visual advantages of structural polychromy that was beloved of the most earnest Gothic revivalists.

ST FEIDHLIMIDH'S CATHEDRAL

BROOKVALE
Railway Road
Cavan
(1845)

The family residence of the building contractor William Hague, whose architect son, William junior, born in 1836, would later establish his career in Cavan before moving to the capital to become a leading ecclesiastical designer to the Catholic Church.

ST AIDAN'S CHURCH

The elaborate capitals of the nave arcade were skillfully formed from hammered metal in a process known as repoussé.

(fig.50)
ST AIDAN'S CHURCH
Main Street,
Butler's Bridge
(1861-3)

The use of banded masonry was then sufficiently novel in Ireland for the Dublin Builder to state erroneously that it was a feature imposed as a result of economy, believing that the architect 'couldn't afford ornament so gained as much effect as possible by contrast of materials'.

ST AIDAN'S CHURCH

Despite the rigours of ecclesiological dogma and the demands of a prolific career, Hague maintained a certain flair for originality and variation that is especially evident in smaller church designs, and can be demonstrated in just three of his gable-fronted designs including the understated and neatly planned St Brigid, Killygalley of 1867, the gaunt, angular, somewhat eccentric St Patrick, Milltown of 1868 and the quietly sophisticated St Patrick, Drumalee, built the same year. As his practice developed in the capital, greater decorative richness became an abiding trait, and is noticeably evident in his larger Cavan churches such as Killeshandra of 1862, Kilnavart of 1866 and Crosserlough of 1888.

(fig.51)
CHURCH OF THE IMMACULATE CONCEPTION
Hall Street
Kingscourt
(1869-72)

The rich Gothic decoration is taken almost to the point of excess, with buttresses, billet eaves, kneelers, finials and elaborate plate tracery. The broach spire left incomplete for more than a century, was finally built in 2011.

ST BRIGID'S CHURCH
Portaliff or Townparks
(1862-3)

The architect's original design conveys his mastery of composition as well as the high standards of draughtsmanship which attended the architectural practice in the nineteenth century.
Courtesy National Library of Ireland

In accordance with high-Victorian tastes and if resources allowed, decoration was indulged almost to the point of excess, typically with richly foliated carving and showy and expensive materials including polished granite and marble for piers and shafts, elaborate roof trusses, patterned encaustic floor tiles and figurative stained glass. These qualities are displayed in the interiors at Kingscourt *(fig.51)*, Hague's most ambitious church, built to a cruciform plan with aisles and a polygonal chancel. As a prominent architect for the Catholic Church, Hague was also called upon to design St Patrick's Seminary *(fig.52)* in Cavan, in which he was also able to adapt his skills in Gothic architecture to an institutional design. The Poor Clares' Convent in Ballyjamesduff, now the Cavan County Museum, of 1881, is an equally imposing three-storied building though it adopts a more familiar form of institutional Gothic, decidedly understated with great expanses of roughcast walling and sparse stone dressing, relieved principally by big Victorian sashes with plate glass.

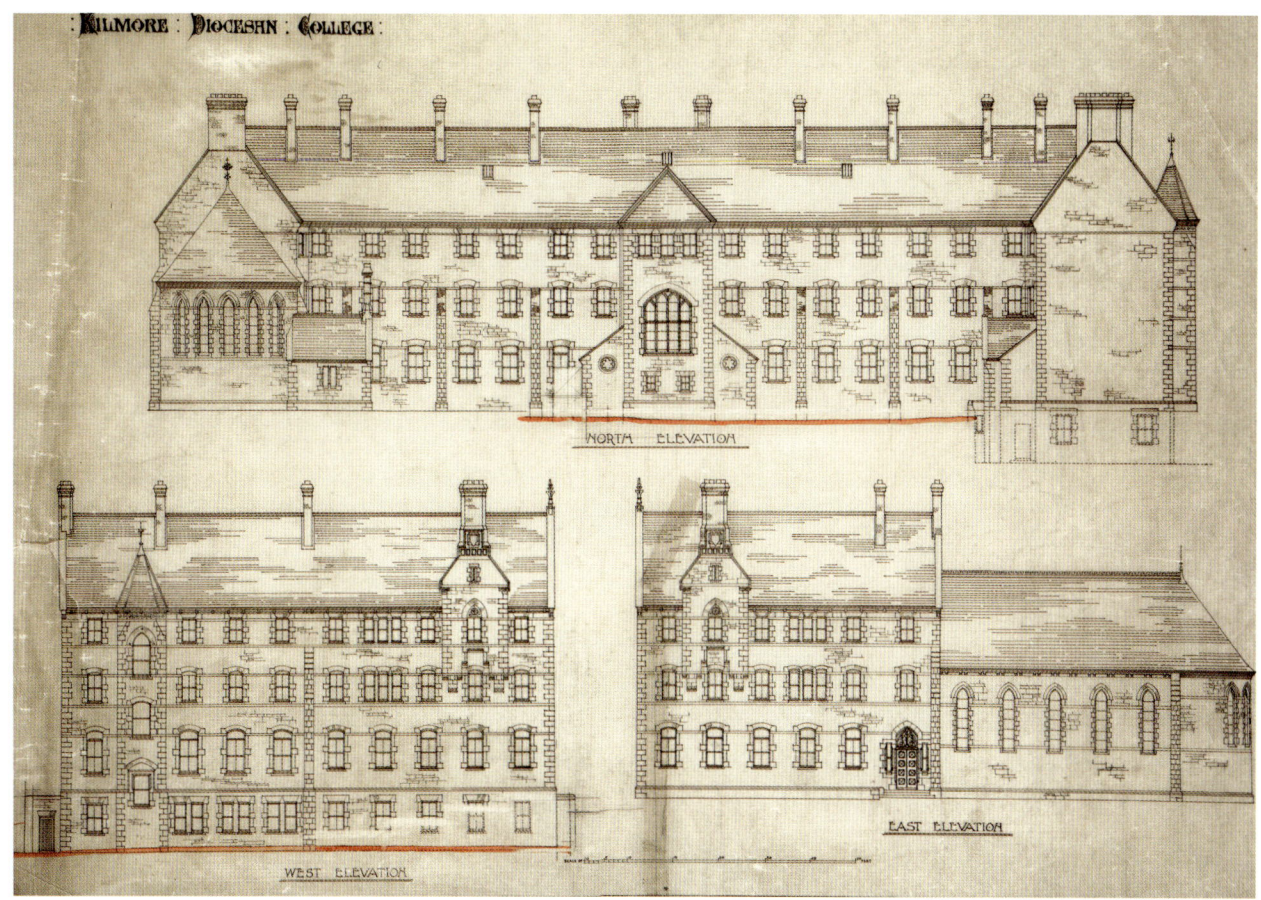

(fig.52)
ST PATRICK'S COLLEGE
Cullies
(c.1870)

In contrast with the subsidiary elevation, shown above, the main facade represents a resolutely symmetrical composition which relies for variety on slender gabled projections and the studied rhythm of the windows, as well as on a carefully distributed display of bold Gothic detailing.
Courtesy Irish Architectural Archive

ST PATRICK'S COLLEGE

Gate and lodge

(fig.53)
JAMPA LING BUDDHIST CENTRE
Owengallees
(c.1850)

Although its architect is unknown, Owendoon, now Jampa Ling Buddhist Centre, represents an accomplished design that is given a highly textured finish and distinctive details.

The appeal of the Gothic Revival to high-Victorian tastes made it increasingly influential amongst all building types and encouraged architects to adopt a more eclectic approach in their exploration of the possibilities of the style. Owendoon *(fig.53)*, a mildly Italianate house built for George L'Estrange, is by far the most innovative example reflecting this trend amongst country-house designers, and remarkable for its interesting blend of Gothic and Moorish elements, clearly inspired by the influential architectural theorist John Ruskin. The boundless limits of invention and rich potential of materials are made strikingly

The Nineteenth Century

(fig.54)
RED LODGE
Cloverhill Demesne
(c.1890)

This simple, polygonal-ended porter's lodge in red brick of c.1800, attributable to Francis Johnston, was wildly transformed into a beguiling two-storey house, fancifully conceived like a gingerbread house with timbered oriel dormer and an open porch.

(fig.55)
BAILIEBOROUGH LODGE
Market Square
Bailieborough
(1878)

The predominantly red-brick façade of this former Presbyterian Institute was given great vibrancy with a zebra-like pattern of red and black around the openings and dressed stone for the quoins.

evident by the transformation of the Red Lodge *(fig.54)* at Cloverhill. The former Presbyterian Institute *(fig.55)* at Bailieborough, now the Masonic Hall, displays the most spirited use of polychromy of any building in Cavan.

(fig.56)
ALLIED IRISH BANK
Market Street
Cootehill
(1858)

It adopts the character of a Renaissance palazzo, successfully combining classical and Gothic elements of fifteenth-century Florentine and Venetian architecture to achieve a highly sophisticated design.

Economic growth rose steadily after the calamity of the Great Famine, and while its pace in Cavan was rather slower than most other places, improved prosperity is reflected in a number of ambitious mercantile buildings. Of the few banks built in the county in the nineteenth century, the former Provincial Bank (AIB) *(fig.56)* at Cootehill is undoubtedly the finest, and amongst the best works of the company architect, William G. Murray. In 1862 William Hague was the architect for the same company at its premises *(fig.57)* on Farnham Street, a rare secular work by him.

(fig.57)
FORMER PROVINCIAL BANK
Farnham Street
Cavan
(1862)

The design adopts the form of a typical three-storey-over-basement town house, which has been richly dressed up in stucco with mannered or quirky classical devices, especially on its upper floors.

The Nineteenth Century

(fig.58)
D. JAMESON MEDICAL HALL
Main Street
Bailieborough
(c.1780)

For the most part, the architectural character of business premises remained straightforward, largely governed by the practical qualities and the proportions of classical architecture whose orderly designs perfectly accomodated the requirements of advertising and display. Although early shopfronts are extremely rare, some important later examples survive to attest to the strong architectural interest and variety that existed amongst the drapers, grocers, chemists and publicans. The simplicity of the Tuscan order was especially favoured, seen to good effect on the Medical Hall *(fig.58)* in Bailieborough and Paddy Fox's *(fig.59)* premises in Mullagh, where in each case the idea of the classical entablature provides a generous frieze for the nameboard while thin, panelled pilasters support it and are widely spaced so as to frame generous window displays in a symmetrical composition.

MC BRIDE'S BAR
Market Street
Ballyjamesduff
(1816)

An excellent example of another type of shopfront popular from the Victorian era that still endures today, composed as an asymmetrical design in which the pilasters rise to rich foliated brackets that support the signboard.

(fig.59)
PADDY FOX
Main Street
Mullagh
(c.1870)

BOYLAN'S
Main Street
Kilnaleck
(1871)

The plain rubble walls are nicely contrasted with the lively painted brick trim to the windows, while the ground floor is arranged with a pleasing irregularity: the well-composed shopfront set to the side where its pilasters are decorated with shamrock motifs.

J MC BARRON
Main Street
Ballyconnell
(c.1850)

Slender pilasters with subtle brackets, frame an attractive symmetrical design, and support a simple nameboard which retains its raised lettering, attractively painted to imitate marble and an extremely rare survival of a once common type.

(fig.60)
COOTEHILL RAILWAY STATION
Killycramph
(1860-1)
On the opposite front, the steep slate roof attractively sweeps down between the gables to form an open veranda, supported on slender cast-iron columns, offering a pleasing ornamental display of a material that was widely exploited in almost every aspect of railway engineering
Courtesy Cavan County Library

Improvement in trade was greatly enhanced by the transport infrastructure in the county, and efforts to open up the difficult lakeland terrain began when works were initiated on the Erne system in 1846 to create a navigation connecting the Shannon with the Ulster Canal. The completion of the Ballinamore to Ballyconnell waterway in 1858 as a summit canal, designed by the engineer William T. Mulvany, represented one of the most ambitious engineering projects undertaken within the region, though its commercial success and viability would quickly be eclipsed by railway, which rapidly became central to the economic development of the provinces. The railways also made a vital contribution to the growing complexity of the architectural tradition in Cavan, as each of the various companies built noticeably individual stations by using diverse styles. Although all its railways lines have fallen into disuse, the surviving stations with their solidly built goods sheds and locomotive houses, and their attendant features such as signal boxes and bridges, all affirm the engineering triumphs of the age. This transport innovation was first brought to Cavan by the Midland & Great Western Railway, for whom George Wilkinson in 1855 designed the handsomely modest station at Crossdoney, choosing an assured Italianate style, which he also adopted for the larger and plainer terminus in Cavan of 1862. William G. Murray opted for a severe twin-gabled Gothic design for his station at Cootehill **(fig.60)**, built for the Dundalk & Enniskillen Railway Company.

After the smaller standard-gauge railway companies became amalgamated under the Great Northern Railway, its chief engineer, William H. Mills, became responsible for the later Victorian stations, designing Belturbet **(fig.61)** in 1885, a well-preserved station in a understated Italianate style. The station was shared by the narrow gauge Cavan & Leitrim Railway, established in the 1880s, and as the buildings designed by Mills were usually distinguished by the use of polychrome brickwork, it is possible that he was also responsible for the stations at Bawnboy Road and Ballyconnell, which adopt the same lively facades.

(fig.61)
BELTURBET RAILWAY STATION
Chapel Road
Belturbet
(1887)

The long single-storey façade is terminated at one end by the two-storied stationmaster's house.

RAILWAY BRIDGE
Straheglin
(1885)

An Introduction to the Architectural Heritage of County Cavan

CAVAN TOWN HALL

With its tall proportions and unusual massing it provides a fitting authority to its purpose, even if its side street location deprives it of a dominant presence in the town.
Courtesy Irish Architectural Archive

The Twentieth Century

(fig.62)
CAVAN TOWN HALL
Town Hall Street
Cavan
(1909)

The use of stone gives an appealing ruggedness befitting the kind of informality found in the vernacular tradition, while the articulation of the surfaces, the turret-like projections and use of casement windows invest it with an almost medieval quality, leading contemporaries to think of it as a neo-Norman design.

CAVAN TOWN HALL

Staircase detail.

While radical change characterised the political events of the early twentieth century, the building traditions in Cavan remained largely unaffected, standing aloof, like much of Irish architecture, from the revolutionary ideals disseminated by the rise of the modern style. Not with standing this, one of the most engaging and original buildings of the early twentieth century found anywhere in Ireland is the town hall *(fig.62)* in Cavan, a masterpiece by William Alphonsus Scott, inspired by the arts and crafts ideals of the influential English designer William Morris. The movement advocated a return to traditional values and prized the informal virtues of individual creativity and the methods of the craftsman over the rigid mundaneness that was gradually being imposed on design by mass-production.

BELTURBET TOWN HALL
The Diamond
Belturbet
(1928)

When the Georgian town hall was demolished in 1927, the Cavan architect Patrick J. Brady designed a more modest replacement, with simplified classical details that were stylised in a vaguely arts and crafts manner.

RIVER LODGE
Drumloaghan
(1932)

Evoking the charms of English domestic architecture in a Tudor-inspired cottage design attributed to William M. Mitchell & Sons, the lodge's gabled fronts, attractively irregular with sweeping roofs, offer a satisfying mix of materials using tile-cladding, half-timbering and masonry walling.

(fig.63)
BELTURBET POST OFFICE
Bulter Street
Belturbet
(1904)

The rusticated baroque doorcase with its bottle-like columns and scrolled pediment is particularly striking.

(fig.64)
BANK OF IRELAND
Main Street
Cavan
(1907)

The bank adopts a tall and imposing Italianate design, with vigorous limestone detailing including open balustraded parapets, modillion cornice and matching entrances on the ground floor framed by a simple Tuscan order.

Scott absorbed many of these ideas, and in this work fused traditional methods with innovative design that continues to reference ideas from the past.

Most Edwardian architects adhered firmly to old traditions, continuing to engage closely with historical styles, aware that architecture, like language, contained a rich vocabulary that offered a wellspring for creative and original ideas. Consequently the classical orders continued to be brought alive, often with designs that evoked the vigorous and mannered classicism found in European baroque architecture. The post office **(fig.63)** at Belturbet, adopting the usual livery of red brick and dressed limestone favoured by its architects Robert Cochrane and George William Crowe of the Office of Public Works, is a fanciful and quirky small building with shaped gables and an ebullient baroque doorcase.

The palazzo type which had become a reliable staple for the banking companies in the

nineteenth century, with its appealing connotations of solidity and security, endured into the twentieth century. It was given widespread expression in Cavan as population decline began to moderate for the first time since the Famine, leading to a strong commercial revival. That growing commercial confidence is displayed in the former Hibernian Bank *(fig.64)* in Cavan of 1907 by Edward J. Toye and the nearby Ulster Bank of 1911 by Blackwood & Jury, both assured Italianate compositions whose red brick and limestone carries on a combination that was widely favoured amongst late-Victorian designers. The stuccoed former Northern Bank in Bailieborough of 1912 by G.W. Ferguson is a more moderate Italianate design, and one that could just as easily have been produced decades before.

The prolific firm of W.H. Byrne & Son adopted a pleasing neo-Georgian idiom in its work for the Hibernian Bank in Cavan of the 1920s, which was employed in a no-nonsense manner at Bailieborough *(fig.65)* where the ordered five-bay stuccoed front was given a handsome ashlared porch, and in a more frivolous way at Kingscourt *(fig.66)*.

BALLYJAMESDUFF GARDA STATION
Granard Street
Ballyjamesduff
(1935)
Later public works built following the establishment of the newly independent Irish state, which included schools and Garda stations, adopted a simple evocation of Georgian architecture, no doubt favoured for its practical efficiency as well as its aesthetic charm.

The Twentieth Century

(fig.65)
BANK OF IRELAND
Main Street
Bailieborough
(1924)

A well-ordered five-bay façade in smooth render and a handsome porch finely executed in limestone.
Courtesy Irish Architectural Archive

(fig.66)
BANK OF IRELAND
Main Street
Kingscourt
(1922)

This neo classical design evokes the work of Robert Adam in the display of delicate urns and swags over the windows, a somewhat frivolous treatment contrasting with the more reassuringly stern countenance usually given to bank buildings.
Courtesy Irish Architectural Archive

(fig.67)
CHURCH OF THE SACRED HEART
Arvagh
(1927-9)

This large church represents an assured design conceived in an Italian-Romanesque style, striking for its twin-towered Lombardic front.

(fig.68)
ST MICHAEL'S CHURCH
Station Road
Cootehill
(1927-30)

A large and robust Gothic-revival church built fully in the nineteenth-century tradition with accomplished architectural detailing, the work of the contractor James Wynne.

The seriousness of this architectural firm's approach to the value of historicism is made clearer in its commissions for the Catholic Church, whose building campaigns continued apace over the course of the century. Their 1927 designs for Arvagh *(fig.67)* and Cootehill *(fig.68)* show a capacity to work competently and with ease in either a Gothic or classical idiom, displayed in each church on large and imposing buildings that carry on nineteenth-century building practices with their use of traditional materials and the quality of workmanship.

SS PATRICK AND FELIM
Courtesy Irish Architectural Archive

The key figure in the practice was Ralph Byrne whose erudition and command of architectural vocabulary were displayed in three major churches of the 1930s, designed for Mullingar, Athlone and Cavan. The Cathedral of SS Patrick and Felim *(fig.69)* was the last of these, built on an elevated site with a soaring steeple, and possessing a degree of stately magnificence that was rarely displayed in twentieth-century buildings in Ireland. Its great Corinthian portico employs the architecture of Rome to invest the building with great religious and civic power.

(fig.69)
SS PATRICK AND FELIM
Farnham Street
Cavan
(1939-42)
An architectural tour de force for its erudite handling of the classical vocabulary, which includes references to the architecture of Palladio and Gibbs. The use of granite with Portland stone is noteworthy, reflecting a tradition established by the finest public buildings in Dublin.

The Twentieth Century

(fig.70)
HOUSE
Gallonbulloge or Blackbull
(c.1910)

This roadside house retains all the pleasing ingredients of vernacular architecture. A portion of its ground floor originally served as a small rural shop.

In contrast, the everyday buildings of the countryside held fast to the pleasing simplicity of the vernacular traditions, represented in countless roughcast and slate-roofed houses and rural shops. These are perfectly exemplified by the trim roadside house at Gallonbulloge *(fig.70)* with its easy composure and by the crossroads building at Lisnabantry *(fig.71)*, where the L-plan building forms a welcoming apron to the front. The more unassuming house at Lisnaclea *(fig.72)* captures the quiet sense of the Cavan countryside that prevailed through much of the twentieth century.

(fig.71)
P. MORGAN
Lisnabantry
(c.1820, c.1900)

In the manner typical of many rural shops, this well-preserved group of buildings stands prominently at a rural crossroads and was once an important focus in the life of the rural community. Fortunately, although it is no longer in use as a shop, its small shopfront remains intact.

(fig.72)
HOUSE
Lisnaclea
(c.1910)

The corrugated-iron structure standing nearby was once a rural shop and a focus for community life.

THE ARCADE
Main Street
Kilnaleck
(c.1820, c.1950)

The streamlined elegancies of the art deco style are captured in this rare vitrolite and chrome shopfront.

The Twentieth Century

By the 1950s new buildings continued to be dominated by commissions from a vibrant Catholic Church, though ambition and innovation was increasingly restrained by the need for economy. W.H. Byrne & Sons continued to be favoured, their work represented by the parish churches of Drung **(fig.73)** and Belturbet with nominal classical and Romanesque details that characterise the designs produced after Ralph Byrne's death by his nephew Simon Aloysius Leonard. References to historical styles gradually abated and were effectively abandoned before the end of the following decade in the Church of Our Lady of Lourdes **(fig.74)** at Ballyconnell. The same basic format of hall and offset tower was retained for this church, which is otherwise distinct principally for its warehouse-like proportions and the predominant use of concrete, mostly in the form of coarsely

(fig.73)
CHURCH OF THE IMMACULATE CONCEPTION
Drung
(1947-8)

This bulky stuccoed hall with its slender offset tower is typical of the 1950s work of Simon Aloysius Leonard of W.H.Byrne & Son.

(fig.74)
OUR LADY OF LOURDES CHURCH
Ballyconnell
(1968)

The use of coarse concrete blocks and faceted panels on the main front invest the walls with a strong textural quality.

(fig.75)
ST JOSEPH'S CHURCH
Virginia Road
Ballyjamesduff
(1966)

The structural potential of concrete was fully exploited here to create the extraordinary mesh-like window that fills the centre of the façade.

ST JOSEPH'S CHURCH

Interior

ST BRIDGET'S CHURCH
Larah
(1983)

An irregularly planned church that is striking for the novel wedge-shaped roofs denoting the entrance and sanctuary on opposing sides of the building.

pulvinated blocks that invest the walls with a strong textural quality. The same angular profile attends the church at Ballyjamesduff *(fig.75)* by Philip Cullivan built in brown brick and concrete. The complete rejection of historical references in accordance with modernist principles became more mainstream in the 1970s as the building programme of the Catholic Church continued in the new post-Vatican II era, with new building replacing old strictly along utilitarian lines to satisfy the requirements of liturgical reform. This is evident in the buildings at Termon and Killyconnan, both built with a specific emphasis on creating bright open plans for inclusive worship, which results in unusual structural forms impossible to reconcile with a traditional building typology.

At the beginning of the twenty-first century the guiding principles of modernism continue to dominate in new building design, holding the same fascination for architects who endeavour to explore the limits of style-less buildings and are keen to experiment with new materials. The Johnston Central Library *(fig.76)* in Cavan, designed by Shaffrey Associates, reflects this approach.

(fig.76)
JOHNSTON LIBRARY
Farnham Street
Cavan
(2004)

A building of functional design, whose bulky massing in angular forms and array of machined materials all boldly intrude on the more conventional complexion of the historic environment.

JOHNSTON LIBRARY

Interior

AN INTRODUCTION TO THE ARCHITECTURAL HERITAGE *of* COUNTY CAVAN

LAWSON'S FORD BRIDGE

Annaghlee
(c.1750)

Conclusion

The places of Cavan, as with everywhere, are greatly defined by the built heritage they contain. The accretion of buildings on a landscape over time represents a rich cultural resource, telling us not just about changing building traditions and styles but about the nature of developments within societies, giving a perspective on everyday life and attitudes in the past. For much of the modern age, the enduring character of Cavan was one of small-farm landscapes amongst its small picturesque hills and lakelands, with modest farmhouses sheltered in farmyards in a patchwork of fields and hedgerows. While rural mills and crossroad smithies have almost entirely fallen silent in this modern age, working farms endure and many old farms have been adapted to modernity without loss of attractiveness; historic churches continue to bind rural communities, intrinsic to family heritage and sense of place. This vernacular landscape of quiet tradition has in so many ways been carried forward successfully into the twenty-first century.

The impacts of modernity have of course been greater within the urban environment. Although churches, schoolhouses, shops, public houses and street terraces still define the core texture of historic towns, rapid demographic growth and unparalleled economic prosperity have imposed a disproportionate quantity of new buildings over a very short period.

With homogeneity widespread amongst modern building practices, we have greater cause to value the rich diversity of the past. One constant in this era of change has been the endurance of the built heritage of Cavan. Each of the buildings celebrated in this book, whether represented by the monumental or the seemingly mundane, is unique to the place to which it belongs. The historic buildings of Cavan are bound to enrich the lives of everyone who encounters them and so deserve to be passed on in good order to the future.

An Introduction to the Architectural Heritage *of* County Cavan

FORMER METHODIST CHURCH AND MANSE
Bridge Street,
Cootehill
(1868)

Further Reading

Bardon, Jonathan, *A History of Ulster*, Belfast: Blackstaff Press, 1992

Brett, Charles E. B., *Court Houses and Market Houses of the Province of Ulster*, Belfast: Ulster Architectural Heritage Society, 1973

Coote, Charles, *Statistical Survey of the County of Cavan*, Dublin: Graisberry and Campbell, 1802

Cumann Seanchais Bréifne, *Bréifne*, Cavan: Cumann Seanchais Bhréifne, 1958 -

Davies, Oliver, 'The Castles of County Cavan', Parts 1 & 2 in *Ulster Journal of Archaeology*, Vol. 11, Belfast: Ulster Archaeological Society, 1947

Davies, Oliver, 'The Churches of County Cavan' in *Journal of Royal Society of Antiquaries of Ireland*, Vol. 78, Dublin: Royal Society of Antiquaries of Ireland, 1948

Day, Angelique and McWilliam, Patrick (eds.), *Ordnance Survey Memoirs of Ireland, Counties of South Ulster 1834-8*, Belfast: Institute of Irish Studies in association with the Royal Irish Academy, 1996

Deane, J.A.K., *The Gate Lodges of Ulster*, A Gazetteer, Belfast: Ulster Architectural Heritage Society, 1994

Gillespie, Raymond (ed.), *Cavan: Essays on the History of an Irish County*, Blackrock: Irish Academic Press, 2004

Gould, Michael H., *The Workhouses of Ulster*, Belfast 9: Ulster Architectural Heritage Society, 1983

Rev. G. Hill, *An historical account of the Plantation of Ulster at the commencement of the seventeenth century, 1608-20*, Belfast: McCaw, Stevenson & Orr, 1877

R.J. Hunter, 'Towns in the Plantation of Ulster' in *Studia Hibernica*, No. 11, Baile Átha Cliath, Coláiste Phádraig, 1971

Kevin J. James, *Handloom Weavers in Ulster's Linen Industry 1815-1914*, Dublin: Four Courts Press, 2007

S.K. Kirker, 'Cloughoughter Castle, County Cavan' in *Journal of the Royal Society of Antiquaries of Ireland*, Vol. 21, Dublin: Royal Society of Antiquaries of Ireland, 1890-91

Lawrence Kirkpatrick, *Presbyterians in Ireland, An illustrated History*, Holywood, Co. Down: Booklink, 2006

Kevin V. Mulligan, *South Ulster: the counties of Armagh, Cavan and Monaghan*, London: Yale University Press, 2013

Patrick O'Donovan, *Archaeological Inventory of County Cavan*, Dublin Stationery Office, 1995

Jeremy Williams, *A Companion Guide to Architecture in Ireland 1837-1921 Blackrock*, Co.Dublin, Irish Academic Press, 1994

Registration Numbers

The structures mentioned in the text are listed below. Further information on structures in the survey can be found on the website *www.buildingsofireland.ie* by searching with the Registration Number. The structures below are listed by page number. Please note that most of the structures included in this book are privately owned and are not open to the public. However, structures marked with an asterisk (*) which include public buildings, museums and commercial properties are normally accessible.

Page	Structure	Location	Reg. No.
6	Woodlawn	Crover	40403808
6	House	Coppanagh	40403410
7	St Joseph's Church *	Corlea	40402901
7	Dowra Bridge *	Dowra	40400506
8	Drumlane	Milltown	Not included in survey
9	Dual Tomb *	Cohaw	Not included in survey
9	Crannog/Ringfort *	Drummally East	Not included in survey
9	Tomregan Church *	Doon	40304001
11	Knockatemple Castle	Knockatemple	Not included in survey
11	Moybologue Castle	Moybologue	Not included in survey
11	Relagh Beg Castle	Relagh Beg	Not included in survey
11	Castle Rahan	Castlerahan	Not included in survey
11	Kilmore Motte	Kilmore Upper	Not included in survey
11	Belturbet Motte	Belturbet	Not included in survey
11	Cloughoughter Castle	Lough Oughter	Not included in survey
12	Trinity Island	Lough Oughter	Not included in survey
12	Drumlane	Milltown	Not included in survey
12	St Mogue's Church *	Templeport	Not included in survey
12	Lough Annagh Church *	Annagh	Not included in survey
12	Kilmore Old Cathedral *	Kilmore Upper	40402528
14	Relagh Beg Church *	Relagh Beg	Not included in survey
15	Tullymongan Castle	Tullymongan	Not included in survey
15	Tonymore Castle	Tonymore	Not included in survey
15	Castle Cosby	Kevit Upper or Castlecosby	Not included in survey
15	Dun an Rí	Comney	Not included in survey
15	House	Ballymagauran	Not included in survey
16	Belturbet Castle	Belturbet	Not included in survey
16	Bawnboy Castle	Bawnboy	Not included in survey
17	The Garden House	Farnham	40402008
18	St Mary's Church *	Church St, Belturbet	40307022
19	Kilmore Old Cathedral *	Kilmore Upper	Reg. 40402528
21	Killeshandra Old Church *	Church St, Killeshandra	40309001
21	Killeshandra Old Church *	Church St, Killeshandra	40309002
22	Farren Connell	Bobsgrove	40404203
22	Bellamont	Bellamont Forest	40401715
26	Annaghlee	Annaghlee	Not included in survey
26	Ballyhaise House	Drumcrow	40401620
29	Lismore Castle	Lismore Demesne	40402513
30	Ballyhaise Bridge *	Drumcrow	40401623
30	O'Daly's Bridge *	Edenburt	40404402
31	Ballyconnell Castle	Ballyconnell	40304008
31	Castle Hamilton	Killeshandra	40309017
31	Belville House	Belville	Not included in survey
31	Farnham House *	Farnham	40402008
31	Rathkenny House	Rathkenny	40401632
31	Red Hills House	Red Hills	Not included in survey
31	Kilmore Palace	Kilmore Upper	Not included in survey
31	Fleming's Folly	Belville	Not included in survey
33	Rathkenny Tea House	Dernaskeagh	40401743
33	Red Hills House	Red Hill	40401601
33	Ballyconnell Castle	Ballyconnell	40304007
33	B. O'Reilly *	Main St, Bailieborough	40303015

33 Market House
    Main St, Kingscourt
    Not included in survey

35 Central Stores *
    Main St, Kingscourt
    40310015

35 Gartlan's *
    Main St, Kingscourt
    40310020

36 King's Cottage
    Chapel Rd, Bailieborough
    40303029

37 Barn
    Kilnavert
    40401307

38 Rose Cottage
    Killygowan
    40402003

38 Knocknalosset House
    Knocknalosset
    40402311

39 Ricehill
    Coolnagor or Ricehill
    40402503

39 Cavan Abbey *
    Abbey St, Cavan
    40000371

40 Drumloman Church *
    Bracklagh
    40404101

40 Tomregan Church *
    Doon
    Reg. 40304001

42 Holy Trinity Church *
    Kildoagh
    40400913

44 Croaghan Presbyterian Church *
    Coolnashinny or Croaghan
    40401903

45 Corglass Presbyterian Church *
    Lisgar
    40402805

46 Farnham St, Cavan
    Reg. 40000116-19

46 Erskine Terrace, Cavan
    40000089-91

47 Market House *
    The Square, Balljamesduff
    40305005

47 Market House *
    Main St, Ballinagh
    40306009

47 Market House *
    Market Sq, Bailieborough
    40303009

47 16 Farnham St, Cavan
    40000121

48 Distillery House
    Mill Walk, Belturbet
    40307021

49 Drumhillagh Mill
    Drumhillagh
    40402320

49 Lifeforce Mill
    River St, Cavan
    40001069

50 Cavan Courthouse *
    Farnham St, Cavan
    40000106

51 Cootehill Courthouse *
    Market St, Cootehill
    40308002

52 Bailieborough Courthouse *
    Main St, Bailieborough
    40303002

52 All Saint's Church *
    Market St, Cootehill
    40308001

52 Lurgan Church *
    Main St, Virginia
    40311007

52 Mullagh Church *
    Mullagh
    40404009

53 Cavan Church of Ireland
    Church *
    Farnham St, Cavan
    40000114

54 Church of the Immaculate
    Conception *
    Chapel Lane, Kingscourt
    40310021

54 St Ultan's *
    Killinkere
    Not included in survey

54 St Joseph's Church *
    Corlea
    40402901

54 St Mark's Church of Ireland
    Church *
    Larah
    40402111

54 Munterconnaught Church *
    Knockatemple
    40404303

54 Derryland Church of Ireland
    Church *
    Aghnacor
    40402403

54 Dernakesh Church of Ireland
    Church *
    Dernakesh
    40402205

54 St Anne's Church *
    Virginia Rd, Bailieborough
    40303026

56 Killeshandra Church *
    Portaliff Glebe
    40309008

56 Christ Church *
    Old Virginia Rd, Ballyjamesduff
    40305006

56 Bailieborough Church of Ireland
    Church *
    Church St, Bailieborough
    40303001

56 Ballyjamesduff Methodist
    Church *
    Market St, Ballyjamesduff
    40305002

56 Blacklion Methodist Church *
    Blacklion
    40400206

56 Ballyconnell Methodist Church *
    Main St, Ballyconnell
    40304003

56 Cavan Presbyterian Church *
    Farnham St, Cavan
    40000086

59 St Patrick's Church *
    Shercock
    40402328

59 Former St Mary's Church *
    Virginia
    40311013

59 Old Church *
    Ballyconnell
    40401004

60 St Mary's Church *
    Kilconny
    40401502

61 Knipe Mausoleum *
    Widow's House Lane, Belturbet
    40307032

61 Philip Smith Memorial *
    St Felim's Church, Ballinagh
    40306011

62 Farnham House *
    Farnham
    40402008

62 Cloverhill House
    Cloverhill Demesne
    40401507

62 Royal School
    College St, Cavan
    40000142

64 Farnham Schools
    Farnham St, Cavan
    40000168

64 Mill Vale
    Cornagarrow
    40401722

65 Killinagh Glebe
    Termon
    40400203

65 Kildallon Glebe
    Bocade Glebe
    40401421

67 Tullyvin House
    Tullyvin
    40401727

67 Templeport House
    Port
    40400914

67 Cabra Castle *
    Cormey
    40403506

68 Cabra Castle *
    Cormey
    40403507

69 Castle Saunderson
    Castle Saunderson Demesne
    40401110

70 Castle Saunderson Church *
    Castle Saunderson Demesne
    40401114

70 Rathkenny House Rakenny 40401632	78 Mountain View Kilsallagh 40400908	84 Poor Clare's Convent * Virginia Rd, Ballyjamesduff 40305009	93 Ballyconnell Railway Station Ballyconnell 40401005
70 See House Kilmore Upper 40402505	79 House Behernagh 40404305	86 Jampa Ling Buddhist Centre Owengallees 40400912	93 Railway Bridge * Straheglin 40307031
70 Kilnacrott House Kilnacrott 40403813	81 St Feidhlimidh's Cathedral * Kilmore Upper 40402505	86 Bailieborough Lodge No.796 Market Sq, Bailieborough 40303011	95 Cavan Town Hall * Town Hall St, Cavan 40000122
71 Corravahan Corravahan 40402103	81 Brookvale Railway Rd, Cavan 40301453	86 Red Lodge Cloverhill Demesne 40401521	96 Belturbet Town Hall * The Diamond, Belturbet 40307017
72 Killykeen Cottage * Killykeen 40402025	81 Quivvy Church Quivvy 40401103	88 Allied Irish Bank * Market St, Cootehill 40308024	96 River Lodge Drumloaghan 40401708
73 Park Hotel/Virginia Lodge * Ballyjamesduff Rd, Virginia 40311001, 40311006	81 St John's Church * Cloverhill 40401508	88 Former Provincial Bank Farnham St, Cavan 40000108	97 Belturbet Post Office * Bulter St, Belturbet 40307016
74 Park Hotel/Virginia Lodge * Ballyjamesduff Rd, Virginia 40311004	81 St Aidan's Church * Main St, Butler's Bridge 40401518	89 D. Jameson Medical Hall * Main St, Bailieborough 40303016	98 Bank of Ireland * Main St, Cavan 40000335
74 Estate Houses Virginia Not included in survey	81 Cavan Methodist Church * Farnham St, Cavan 40000086	89 Paddy Fox * Main St, Mullagh 40404407	98 Ulster Bank * Main St, Cavan 40000256
75 Portlongfield School Portlongfield 40401911	83 St Brigid Church * Killygalley 40402105	90 Mc Bride's Bar * Market St, Ballyjamesduff 40305003	98 Former Northern Bank Main St, Bailieborough 40303025
75 Drumcoghill Church Hall * Drumcoghill 40402420	83 St Patrick's Church * Milltown 40401412	91 Boylan's * Main St, Kilnaleck 40403802	98 Ballyjamesduff Garda Station Granard St, Ballyjamesduff 40305004
76 Kiffagh School Kiffagh 40403208	83 St Patrick Church * Drumalee 40401109	91 J Mc Barron * Main St, Ballyconnell 40304015	98 Bank of Ireland * Main St, Bailieborough 40303023
76 Derrylane School Derrylane 40402402	83 Church Of The Immaculate Conception * Hall St, Kingscourt 40310009	93 Crossdoney Railway Station Crossdoney 40402526	98 Bank of Ireland * Main St, Kingscourt 40310019
76 Cavan Union Workhouse * Cavan 40000445, 40000455	83 St Brigid's Church * Killeshandra 40401915	93 Cootehill Railway Station Killycramph 40401716	100 Church of the Sacred Heart * Arvagh 40302008
76 Bawnboy Union Workhouse Bawnboy 40400907	83 St Patrick's Church * Kilnavert 40401308	93 Cavan Railway Station Cavan 40000452	100 St Michael's Church * Station Rd, Cootehill 40308007
77 Sandy Row Farnham 40402007	83 St Mary's * Crosserlough 40403206	93 Belturbet Railway Station Chapel Rd, Belturbet 40307025	101 SS Patrick and Felim * Farnham St, Cavan 40000113
77 Pair of houses Redhills 40401606	84 St Patrick's College Cullies 40402023	93 Bawnboy Road Railway Station Cloneary 40401305	103 House Gallonbulloge or Blackbull 40402612

103 P. Morgan *
    Lisnabantry
    40402612

103 House
    Lisnaclea
    40402303

103 The Arcade *
    Main St, Kilnaleck
    40403805

105 Church of the Immaculate
    Conception *
    Drug
    40401627

105 Our Lady of Lourdes Church *
    Ballyconnell
    40401004

106 St Joseph's Church *
    Virginia Rd, Ballyjamesduff
    40305008

106 St Bridget's Church *
    Larah
    40402112

107 Johnston Library *
    Farnham St, Cavan
    Not included in survey

CLOVERHILL HOUSE
Cloverhill
(c.1800)

Acknowledgments

Built Heritage and Architectural Policy
Principal Advisor Martin Colreavy

NIAH
Senior Architectural Advisor William Cumming
Architectural Heritage Officer Jane Wales
GIS Technicians Deborah Lawlor, Nadia O'Beirne-Corrigan, Cian O'Connor
NIAH Staff Mildred Dunne, Damian Murphy, TJ O'Meara, Barry O'Reilly
Admin Support Helen Francis, John Knightley, Joan Maher, Suzanne Nally

The NIAH gratefully acknowledges the following in the preparation of the Cavan County Survey and Introduction:

Survey Fieldwork
Lotts Architecture and Urbanism

Recorders
Brian Attley, Desmond Byrne, Sunni Godson, Louise Harrington, Richard McLoughlin, Mike O'Neil, Rosanne Walker

Introduction
Writer Kevin Mulligan
Editor Jane Wales
Copy Editor Lucy Freeman
Photography David O'Shea Photography
Designed by 2b Creative
Printed by Hudson Killeen

The NIAH wishes to thank all those who allowed access to their property for the purpose of the Cavan County survey and subsequent photography.

The NIAH also wishes to acknowledge the generous assistance given by: PJ Dunne, Tom O'Sullivan, Anne-Maire Ward, Lady Farnham, Leslie McKeague, Tony Roche, Irish Architectural Archive, National Library of Ireland

Sources of Illustrations
Original photography by David O'Shea Photography unless otherwise indicated. Ownership of archival images is individually acknowledged. The NIAH has made every effort to source and acknowledge the owners of all archival illustrations included in this Introduction. The NIAH apologies for any omission made, and would be happy to include acknowledgement in future issues of this Introduction.

Please note that the majority of the structures included in the Cavan County Survey are privately owned and are therefore not open to the public.

ISBN: 978-1-4064-2749-3

© Government of Ireland 2013